Get Ready for International Business

English for the workplace

A2

Student's Book 1

Andrew Vaughan
& Dorothy E Zemach

MACMILLAN

Contents

1 Here are some of the companies and characters you will hear and read about. After the Viewpoints section in each unit, complete the information about each person.

UNIT 1

NAME Anna Martinez
JOB ______________
FROM Venezuela

UNIT 1

NAME ______________
JOB Student
FROM England | UK

UNIT 1

NAME Michael Yang
JOB Small business owner
FROM ______________

UNIT 2

NAME ______________
JOB Office worker
FROM ______________

UNIT 12

NAME ______________
JOB Product Planner
FROM ______________

UNIT 12

NAME ______________
JOB ______________
FROM Argentina

UNIT 12

NAME Rajiv Das
JOB ______________
FROM ______________

UNIT 11

NAME Amnuay Chaichen
JOB ______________
FROM ______________

UNIT 10

NAME ______________
JOB ______________
FROM Ukraine

UNIT 10

NAME Mei-ling Chen
JOB Project Manager
FROM ______________

UNIT 9

NAME ______________
JOB ______________
FROM US

UNIT 3

NAME

JOB

FROM Germany

UNIT 3

NAME Emiko Yamaguchi

JOB Banker

FROM

UNIT 4

NAME

JOB Civil Servant

FROM

UNIT 4

NAME Alma Hansson

JOB Accounts Manager

FROM

UNIT 5

NAME

JOB

FROM Korea

UNIT 6

NAME

JOB

FROM France

UNIT 8

NAME

JOB Marketing executive

FROM Brazil

UNIT 8

NAME Lise Martin

JOB

FROM

UNIT 7

NAME Tran Chung Nguyen

JOB

FROM Vietnam

UNIT 7

NAME

JOB Project Manager

FROM

UNIT 1

Let me give you my card

Aims

- Introducing yourself
- Talking about your job
- Giving contact information
- Starting and ending conversations
- Viewpoints: Using business cards
- In business: Your business card

Listen and practise Introducing yourself

1 Describe the photo. Where are the people? What are they doing?

2 1.02 Sarah and Hari are meeting. Listen and write T for true or F for false next to each sentence. Then check your answers with a partner.

a They are meeting for the first time. ______

b They work for the same company. ______

3 1.02 Listen again and complete the conversation. Then practise with a partner. Take turns being Sarah and Hari.

Sarah: Hello. My name's Sarah Cohen. I ___*work*___ ___*for*___ Comet Technologies.

Hari: Hi, Sarah. I'm Hari Kumar. I'm ________ Asia Retailing.
Nice to ________ you.

Sarah: Nice to meet you too. I'm sorry, I didn't ________ your ________ name.

Hari: It's Kumar. Here – let me ________ you my card.

4 Practise the conversation again. Change the information in blue using the names and companies below.

Josh Brown / Brown Construction

Su-yun Kim / Insung Limited

5 1.03 What do you think Sarah and Hari will do next? Tick (✓) your guesses. Then listen to see if you are correct.

a ☐ Sarah will give Hari her business card.

b ☐ Hari will ask for Sarah's phone number.

c ☐ They will talk about their companies.

d ☐ They will talk about their jobs.

Talking about your job

1 Look at the questions and answers about another person's job. Ask and answer the questions with a partner.

A: What do you do?	B: I'm (an Engineer). I'm in (R&D).
A: Who do you work for?	B: I work for (company name).
A: Who are you with?	B: I'm with (company name).
A: Where do you work?	B: I work in (Berlin).

2 Look at the tables. They show ways you can talk about job titles and departments. With a partner or group, add some more.

		Job title
I'm You're He's / She's	a / an	Web Designer / (Department) Manager / Product Planner / Researcher / Sales Assistant / Administrative Assistant / Accountant __________ / __________ .

		Department name
I'm You're He's / She's	in	Information Technology (IT) / Advertising / Human Resources / Marketing / Purchasing / Sales / Research & Development (R&D) __________ / __________ .

3 Complete the sentences using words from the tables above.

a He's *an* *Accountant*

b You're __________ __________

c I'm __________ __________

d She's __________ __________

e He's __________ __________

4 1.04 Listen to the conversation. Then practise with a partner. Take turns being Amanda and Steve.

Amanda: Hello. Are you new here?

Steve: Yes, I just started on Monday.

Amanda: Really? That's great. By the way, my name's Amanda Parker. Please call me Mandy. I'm an Administrative Assistant.

Steve: Nice to meet you, Mandy. I'm Steve Klein.

Amanda: Nice to meet you. What do you do, Steve?

Steve: I'm in Advertising. Well, I'll see you soon.

Amanda: See you.

5 Practise the conversation again. Change the information in blue using your own names and information from exercise 2.

Giving contact information

1 Look at the business card. Take turns reading the numbers and addresses with a partner. Then label the card with words from the box.

area code	country code	post/zipcode	at	dot	underscore

a ______________________

b ______________________

c ______________________

d ______________________

e ______________________

f ______________________

2 1.05 Listen to four conversations. Fill in each business card with the missing information.

A

Fine French Foods
Simply the Best
Sebastien Michel
Overseas ____________ Manager

76 rue St. Martin
Paris, France 75001
+ __ __ (1) 55-89-72-36
____________@aliments.______

B

Max Rosenberg
phone: _ _ _ 555- _ _ _ _
email:

C

Marco Supermarkets
Great Food, Great prices
2-14-83 Minami Aoyama
Minato-___ Tokyo 105-8511
(___ ___) 3578-2111
kimurasay@marco.com
Sayako Kimura
____________ Assistant

D

UNIVERSITY OF DETROIT
Detroit, MI _ _ _ _ _
(313) 555-0134
alfulani@____________

Dr Amina Al-Fulani
____________ Professor

Talk business

Student A, turn to page 84.
Student B, turn to page 96.

Conversation strategy Starting and ending conversations

1 1.06 Listen to and read the conversations below. Which one is between friends? Which one is between people meeting for the first time?

Conversation 1

A: Excuse me. Do you have the time?

B: Yes, it's 11 o'clock.

A: Thank you. By the way, my name's Nancy Chen.

B: Nice to meet you, Nancy. I'm Mary Burns. Are you with Global Exports?

A: No, I work for Snappy Snack Foods. I'm in Marketing. Here, let me give you my card.

B: Thanks. Here's mine. I'm a Sales Representative for Golden Palace. We import Chinese food.

Conversation 2

A: Emily! How are you?

B: Hi, Liz. Really good. Have you heard that I changed jobs?

A: Yeah. Who are you with now?

B: Corporate Training Solutions. I'm in Human Resources. And you?

A: Oh, I'm still a Software Developer with Magix. I really like it.

B: Let me give you my new card.

2 Practise the conversations with a partner.

3 Look at these ways to end conversations. Which ones can be used with conversation 1? With conversation 2?

a A: We should get together sometime.
B: Good idea. I'll call you this weekend, OK? ☐

b A: Well, it was a pleasure meeting you.
B: Good to meet you too. ☐

c A: Anyway, I'd better get going. Tell your brother I said 'hello'.
B: I will. See you! ☐

d A: Well, I see someone I need to talk to. It was nice meeting you.
B: You too. Goodbye. ☐

e A: Well, my train leaves in about an hour. I'd better get going.
B: I hope we meet again sometime. Have a safe trip. ☐

f A: Oh, look at the time!
B: Yes, I've got to go. See you around. ☐

4 Practise all of the endings with a partner.

5 Choose an ending to conversation 1 and conversation 2. Then practise the complete conversations.

Viewpoints Using business cards

1 1.07 Listen to people from three different countries talking about business cards. Tick (✓) the sentences you hear.

Juliana Soares,
Student, England, UK

- I don't have a business card.
- Most of my friends have cards.
- Sometimes people give me their cards.
- I like fancy, colourful cards.
- I keep business cards in my pocket.

Anna Martinez,
Sales Manager, Venezuela

- I give and receive a lot of business cards.
- My cards are in English.
- I like plain white cards.
- It's important to treat cards with respect.
- It's OK to write on them.

Michael Yang,
Small business owner, China

- I have two different business cards.
- I give my card to everyone I meet.
- I give and receive cards with both hands.
- I like simple, clear cards.
- I organise them in a small notebook.

2 Discuss these questions in a small group.

- Which person is most like you (or people from your country)?
- Do you think business cards are important? Why or why not?
- Do you have a business card?
- How often do you receive business cards? Who do you receive them from, and why?

3 Look at these business cards in a small group. Which ones do you like? Which ones don't you like? Explain why. Use the vocabulary below and your own ideas.

(un)attractive (not) easy to read fun (un)interesting (un)professional serious simple

In business Your business card

Scenario: You and your group have been asked to design new business cards for your company. The company can be where you work, or where you would like to work. In the group, you each need to design a card for yourself.

1 Discuss in your group.

- What is the company called?
- What kind of company is it? Small? Large? International?
- What does the company make / do?
- What kinds of jobs are there?
- What are the job titles of you and your group members?
- What contact information do you want to include on the card?

2 Draw a picture of the company logo here.

3 Organise your information onto this card. Include your name and title. Each member of the group should make their own card.

4 When you have finished, introduce yourself to other groups in the class using your new business card. Meet as many people as you can. Remember:

Introduce yourself

↓

Ask them their name and where they work

↓

Tell them your job title and where you work (exchange cards)

↓

Politely end the conversation and move on

UNIT 2

I start work at 8:30

Aims

- Saying where you're from
- Reflecting and reacting
- Describing routines
- Describing schedules
- Viewpoints: Working hours
- In business: Describe your workday

Listen and practise Saying where you're from

1 Describe the photo. What are they doing? What are they saying?

2 1.08 Jeff, Beth and May are meeting in Singapore. Listen and write T for true or F for false next to each sentence. Then check your answers with a partner.

a May and Beth are meeting for the first time. ______

b Beth is from the United States. ______

3 1.08 Listen again and complete the conversation. Then practise in groups of three. Take turns being Jeff, May, and Beth.

Jeff: Beth, ______ ______ ______ May Li. May is in Customer Support. May, ______ ______ Beth Wild. Beth's a Designer for Star Design.

May: Nice to meet you, Beth.

Beth: Nice to meet you too, May. Where ______ ______ ______?

May: I'm from Shanghai, in China. ______ ______ ______?

Beth: I'm from San Diego, in the United States.

4 Practise the conversation again. Change the information in blue using the names and jobs below.

Kimiko Tatsuda
(Nagoya, Japan)

Marketing Assistant
Hasegawa Hotels

Maria Lopez
(Mexico City, Mexico)

Sales Manager
BL Chemicals

Mikel Deuter
(Essen, Germany)

Service Engineer
Ruhr Pipe Manufacturing

Lek Phikul
(Hat Yai, Thailand)

Tour Guide
Tour Asia

Ben Poole
(Manchester, UK)

Product Planner
Timson Watches

5 1.09 What do you think May will say next? Tick (✓) your guesses. Then listen to see if you are correct.

a ☐ Is this your first trip to our office?
b ☐ How old are you, Bethan?
c ☐ What do you do, Beth?
d ☐ Let me give you my card.

Conversation strategy Reflecting and reacting

1 Look at the table. It shows questions you can ask to reflect a question back to the speaker.

What about you?
How about you?
And you?

2 1.10 Listen to the four conversations. How do the speakers reflect the question?

a ______________ you?
b ______________ you?
c ______________ you?
d ______________ you?

3 Ask and answer the questions with a partner.

For example: A: *Where were you born?*
B: I was born in ________ . *How about you?*
A: I was born in ________ .

a Who is your favourite singer?
b Can you play a musical instrument?
c What kind of movies do you like?
d Do you play any sports?
e Where are you from?
f Do you like fish?

4 Look at the table. It shows ways you can react to information.

☺	☺	☹
Wow!	Really?	That's a shame.
That's amazing!	That's interesting.	Oh no!
That's great!	I see.	I'm sorry to hear that.

1.11 Listen and repeat. Say the expressions the same way.

5 Practise with a partner. Take turns reading and reacting. Use the information below and your own ideas.

For example: A: *I'm getting married next week!*
B: *That's great!*

a I'm studying French.

c I lost my train pass.

b I went skiing last weekend.

d I have a bad cold.

Describing routines

1 1.12 Listen to May describe a typical workday. Next to each activity write how often she does these things. Then check your answers with a partner.

every day / most days / some days
once / twice / three times / four times / a day / week / month / year

get up at 6:30	a	*every day*
stop for coffee and a muffin	b	
leave home at 7:30	c	
have a morning meeting	d	
eat a sandwich at my desk	e	
study for an hour	f	

Talk business

Student A, turn to page 85.
Student B, turn to page 97.

2 Practise with a partner. Talk about some things you do.

For example: A: *Most days I drink coffee in the morning. How about you?*
B: *Some days I drink coffee. But I drink tea three or four times a day!*

Describing schedules

1 Look at the table. It shows ways you can talk about schedules.

Preposition	Unit	Examples
on	day	on Monday, on Friday
at	time	at nine o'clock, at 8:30pm
in	month, year, part of day, season	in March, in 2010 in the morning, in spring
from … to …	day, time, month, year	from Monday to Thursday, from 4:00 to 6:00pm from April to June, from 2008 to 2010

2 Put the correct prepositions in the spaces. Check your answers with a partner.

a The meeting starts ______ 10:00am.
b ______ Monday ______ Wednesday I work in our head office.
c ______ the afternoon I have a conference call with the US.
d I take my holiday ______ August.
e Lunchtime is ______ twelve-fifteen ______ one o'clock.
f Men don't need to wear ties ______ summer.
g I joined this company ______ 2007.
h ______ Monday we have a morning meeting.

3 1.13 Listen and complete the schedule.

Hiro Makino: March Business Trip

___/3	**12:05pm**	Shanghai–New York (arrive ______________.)
16/3	______ – ______	Inspect Factory Site
16/3	______________	New York–Dallas
___/3	**9:00am – 10:30pm**	Texas Oil: Presentation
17/3	______________	Dallas–SF
17/3	**5:00pm –** ______	SF Office: interview Lindsey Cole
17/3	______________	Dinner: Dieter Muller (SF Manager)
18/3	______________	SF–Shanghai (arrive 19/3 9:40pm)

4 Write true or false statements about Mr Makino's schedule.
Listen to your partner's statements. Are they true or false?

For example: *Mr Makino is arriving in Shanghai on 18th March. False!*

a ______________________________
____

b ______________________________
____

c ______________________________
____

Viewpoints Working hours

1 Read what these people say about working hours. Answer the questions.

- How many days a week do most people work in your country?
- Do most people work long hours in your country?
- How much holiday do people have in your country?

Maggie Kirk
Office Worker, Australia

I work for a busy property developer in Sydney. I travel a lot, so I'm a telecommuter. This means I can work from home, a hotel, or anywhere. I go to the office once or twice a month for meetings with my boss. I work a 40-hour week, but I can decide my schedule every day. This is good for me because I have two small children. I have four weeks' holiday every year, and I try to take time off in summer when my children are out of school.

Soo-hyun Park,
Administrative Staff, Korea

I start work at 8:30. I work five days a week for eight hours a day, with one hour off for lunch. When we are busy, I work overtime. Sometimes I work on Saturdays. In my first year with the company I had ten days off, but now I have 20 days a year. It's difficult for me to take more than four or five days at one time, because my job is very busy. Most people don't use all their holiday.

Michel Dubois,
Systems Engineer, France

In France, work-life balance is important. I work a 35-hour week from Monday to Friday. We have a flexitime system. I can decide when to come to the office, but I must be there between 10:00am and 3:00pm. In my company there is no overtime. We have five weeks' holiday every year. Many companies in France close for a month in the summer – my company closes for three weeks in August.

2 What is important to you when you look for a job?
Rate these items 1–5 (1 = very important, 5 = not important).

	Friendly colleagues	Flexitime	Interesting work	Long holidays	No overtime	Good salary	Telecommuting
Importance							

3 Talk about your answers in a group.

For example: A: *I think* ________ *is / are very important. How about you?*
B: *I don't think* ________ *is / are important. How about you?*

In business Describe your workday

Scenario: You are visiting your old high school as part of a 'careers day'. You and other people have been asked to talk to the students about a 'Typical Workday'.

1 Choose one of the following jobs (or use your own idea).

restaurant owner	high school teacher	construction worker	fashion designer
IT manager	ballet dancer	research scientist	Your own idea:

2 Complete the table with information about your workday.

Time	Place	Activity

3 Work in groups of three. Take turns describing your workday. When you listen to other group members, remember to react, reflect, and ask questions. Begin like this:

I'm a .... This is a typical workday. From / At .... I . . .

UNIT 3

What does your company do?

Aims

- Giving information
- Asking about company background
- Asking for repetition and spelling
- Describing company business
- Viewpoints: What kind of company?
- In business: Describe your company

Listen and practise Giving information

1 Describe the photo. Where are the people? What are they talking about?

2 1.14 Andy is asking Eva about Euro Tech. Listen and circle the correct answer. Ask and answer the questions with a partner.

a	Was Euro Tech established in 1993?	Yes, it was.	No, it wasn't.
b	Is Euro Tech's head office in Paris?	Yes, it is.	No, it isn't.
c	Does Euro Tech have an office in Tokyo?	Yes, it does.	No, it doesn't.

3 1.14 Listen again and complete the conversation. Then practise with a partner. Take turns being Andy and Eva.

Andy: Can I ask you some questions about Euro Tech?
Eva: Yes, of course.
Andy: ________ ________ ________ the company?
Eva: We were established in 1992.
Andy: I see. And ________ ________ ________ head office?
Eva: In Munich. We also have offices in London and Paris.
Andy: ________ ________ people work for Euro Tech?
Eva: We have 45 full-time employees. 35 people work in our head office, and there are 10 workers in our other offices.

4 Practise the conversation again. Change the names and numbers in blue using the information below.

Company	Established	Employees	Head Office	Offices
Timson Watches	1835	150	Geneva (120)	London (10), New York (20)
Natural Beauty	1994	670	Milan (350)	New York (120), Hong Kong (200)
Tour Asia	2000	104	Singapore (60)	Beijing (20), Seoul (14), Bangkok (10)
Comet Technology	2003	19	Portland (10)	San Francisco (5), San Jose (4)

5 1.15 What do you think Andy will ask next? Tick (✓) your guesses. Then listen to see if you are correct.

a ☐ He will ask Eva where she lives.
b ☐ He will ask about Euro Tech's customers.
c ☐ He will ask Eva about her job.
d ☐ He will ask Eva for her telephone number.

Asking about company background

1 Look at the table. It shows questions you can ask about a company.

What		does	your company	do?
Where		is	your head office?	
When		was	the company	established?
How many	offices employees	do	you	have?

2 1.16 Listen and complete the notes. Then check your answers with a partner.

a

Batang Corp.

Established:

Head office: Kuala Lumpur

Offices:

Employees:

Business: imports and exports goods

b

Insung Ltd.

Established:

Head office:

Offices:

Employees: 1,200

Business: supplies foodstuffs

c

BL Chemicals

Established:

Head office:

Offices: 80

Employees:

Business: produces plastic goods

d

Brown Construction

Established: 1913

Head office:

Offices:

Employees:

Business: designs and builds roads and bridges

3 Look at the examples of long and short answers below.
Then ask and answer the questions about the companies in exercise 2.

When was ________ established?	It was established in (2003). / In (2003).
How many employees does ________ have?	It has (750) employees. / (750).
Where is the head office of ________ ?	The head office is in (Seoul). / In Seoul.
How many offices does ________ have?	It has (four) offices. / (four).

4 Now ask and answer questions about Ruben Steel Corp. with a partner.

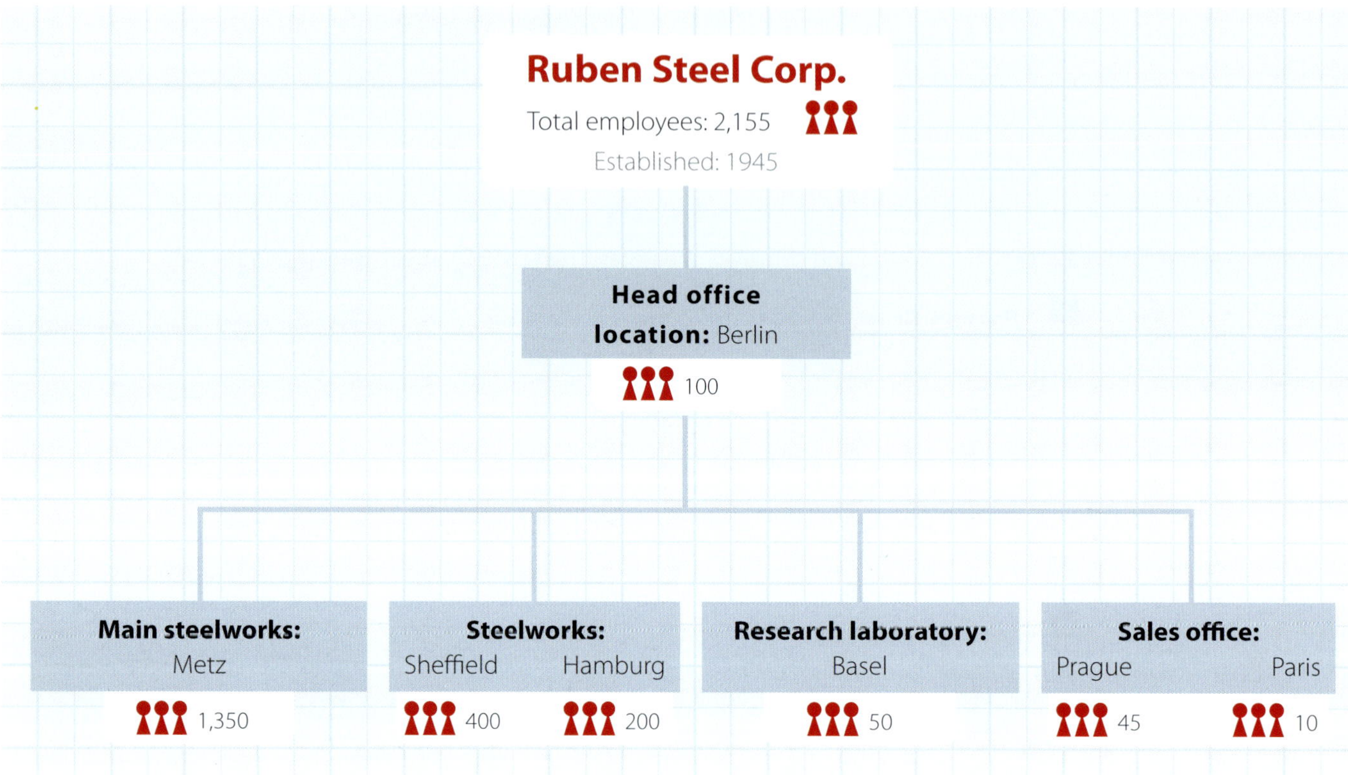

5 Practise with a partner. Student A, give an answer.
Student B, ask the question.

For example: A: *Two.*
B: *How many steelworks does Ruben Steel have?*

B: *In Berlin.*
A: *Where is the head office of Ruben Steel?*

Conversation strategy Asking for repetition and spelling

1 Look at the table. It shows ways you can ask someone to repeat or spell what he or she has said.

I'm sorry,	can you repeat that? can you say that again? can you spell that?	
	can you repeat / spell	your telephone number? the address? your family name?

2 Practise with a partner. Take turns asking the questions.

Talk business

Student A, turn to page 86.
Student B, turn to page 98.

Describing company business

Look at these ways you can talk about what companies do.

Euro Tech **designs** smart phones for the communications industry.

Web Talk **provides** translation of web pages.

1 1.17 Listen and draw a line from the company to the product. Then write the correct words from the box on the lines. You can use some words twice.

builds	develops	manufactures	sells	designs	produces

a Brown Construction *designs and builds*
b Amazon ______
c BL Chemicals ______
d Rockstar ______
e Nisco ______

roads and bridges

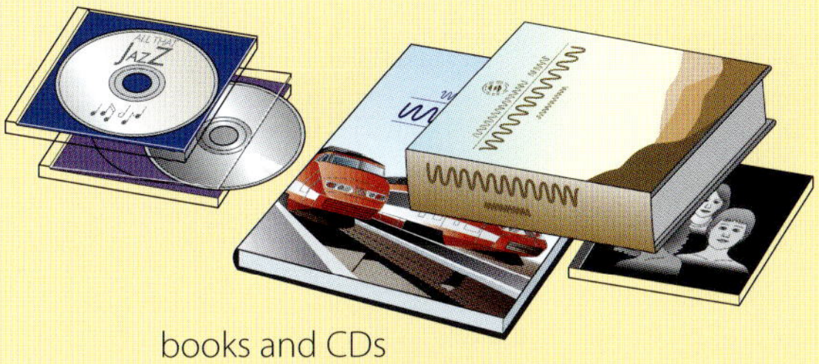

books and CDs

plastic goods

video games

integrated circuits

2 Complete the following sentences using companies you know. Talk about the companies with a partner.

a ______ sells ______.
b ______ makes ______.
c ______.
d ______.
e ______.

3 Ask and answer *yes* / *no* questions with a partner using the information in exercises 1 and 2.

Q: Does ______ sell ______? A: Yes, it does. / No, it doesn't.
Q: Does ______ build ______? A: Yes, it does. / No, it doesn't.

Viewpoints What kind of company?

1 Answer these questions for yourself. Write T for true or F for false next to each sentence. Compare your answers with a partner.

a I want to work for a big company.

b I want to work in a foreign country.

c I want to stay at one company for a long time.

2 1.18 Listen to these people talk about their companies. Match the person with what they say.

☐ My company develops medicines.	☐ I like working for a big company.
☐ I work for a small family company.	☐ Everyone is friendly and I enjoy my job.
☐ We have offices in New York, London and Tokyo.	☐ I need to improve my English!

a Neil Parker,
Pharmacist, US

b George Weber,
Electrical Engineer, Germany

c Emiko Yamaguchi,
Banker, Japan

3 Look at these types of industries. Can you think of any more?

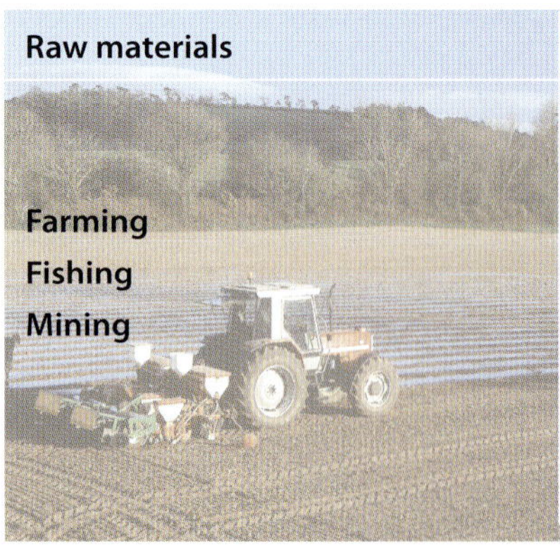

Raw materials

Farming
Fishing
Mining

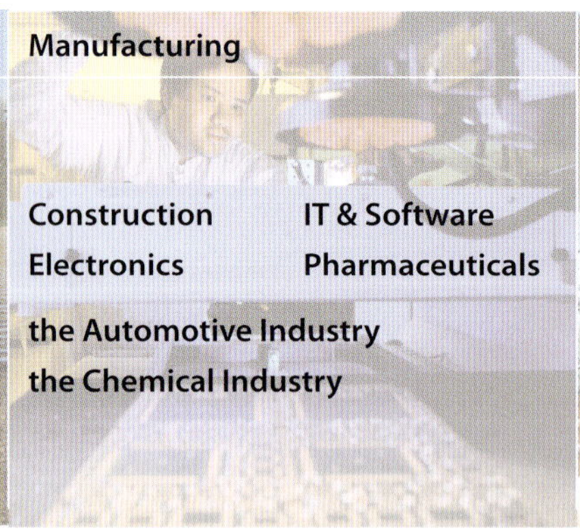

Manufacturing

Construction
IT & Software
Electronics
Pharmaceuticals
the Automotive Industry
the Chemical Industry

Services

Banking
Hospitality
Education
News media
Entertainment
Tourism
Health care
Transportation

4 What kind of industry do you want to work in? Talk about the industries with a small group. Use some of these adjectives or other words you know.

creative difficult exciting interesting challenging well-paid

For example: *I want to work in (the chemical industry) because it's interesting. How about you?*
I want to work in (tourism) because I like to travel. How about you?

In business Describe your company

Scenario: Choose a business you know. A business-focused blog wants to interview someone in your company. Prepare an information sheet so that you are ready to answer questions about the company.

1 Complete the information sheet.

Company name and logo:

Company information:

Established:

Employees:

Head Office:

____

____

____

2 Write down the questions you would like to ask your partner about their company using the information sheet to help you.

3 Take it in turns to be the company representative and the interviewer. Use your information sheet to help you answer the questions. Begin like this:

May I ask you a few questions about your company?

Yes, of course.

UNIT 4

How do you like your job?

Aims

- Making small talk
- Talking about likes and dislikes
- Making suggestions
- Sounding polite
- Viewpoints: Corporate culture
- In business: Company survey

Listen and practise Making small talk

1 Describe the photo. Where are they? What are they doing?

2 1.19 Stefan is talking with Diane. Listen and tick (✓) whether she likes or dislikes these things.

	likes	dislikes
a York	☐	☐
b countryside	☐	☐
c rain	☐	☐

3 1.19 Listen again and complete the conversation. Then practise with a partner. Take turns being Stefan and Diane.

Stefan: Hi, Diane. ________ do you ________ your new job here?
Diane: It's great. And I really like living in York. Although, it ________ rains a lot …
Stefan: It does, but that's why the countryside here is so ________ .
Diane: That's true. I just ________ ________ walking in the rain!

4 1.20 Diane talked about some things she didn't like. How will Stefan respond? Tick (✓) your guesses. Then listen to see if you are correct.

a ☐ He will agree with her.
b ☐ He will talk about something he doesn't like.
c ☐ He will suggest some things for her to buy.
d ☐ He will get angry.

Talking about likes and dislikes

1 To make small talk, people often share their likes and dislikes. Look at the table. It shows ways you can do this. Practise with a partner. Take turns reading the sentences.

	like enjoy	my job. taking business trips.
I	don't mind	our cafeteria.
	don't like can't stand	queuing. commuting.

2 Talk to your partner about some other activities that you like or dislike.

For example: A: *I like baseball. How about you?*

B: *Me too. I like baseball.*

Or

Really? I can't stand baseball.

3 Look at the words in the box below. Are they positive or negative? Put them into the table. Then discuss your choices with a partner, and add some more words to each list.

attractive boring challenging confusing difficult easy exciting frustrating fun interesting

positive

attractive

negative

boring

4 Look at ways you can give more information about likes and dislikes. Practise with a partner. Take turns being A and B.

A: How do you like your job? *(question)*

B: I love it. **It's great**.
It's OK. **It's a little boring**.
Actually, **it's frustrating**.

A: I like our new uniforms. *(statement)*

B: Yeah, me too. **They're attractive**.
Really? Actually, **I can't stand them**!

5 Practise with a partner. Student A: read a question or statement. Student B: respond. Take turns asking and responding in different ways.

Questions
How do you like your new job?
How do you like living here?
How do you like the cafeteria food?
(your own idea)

Statements
I don't like long holidays.
I like working at the weekend.
I like our new computers.
(your own idea)

Making suggestions

1 1.21 When someone talks about something he or she doesn't like, you can make a suggestion. Listen to the sentences in the table. Then practise reading each sentence to a partner.

You should	ask your boss for a day off.
Why don't you	ask your boss for a day off?
I recommend	asking your boss for a day off.
How about	asking your boss for a day off?

2 1.22 Listen to four employees talking about their problems. What suggestion does someone make? Number them in order a–d as you hear them. There are two extra suggestions.

- ☐ I recommend taking an earlier train.
- ☐ Why don't you bring your own lunch?
- ☐ You should talk to your manager.
- ☐ Why don't you ask for more training?
- ☐ You should look for a new job.
- ☐ How about reading the manual?

Talk business

Student A, turn to page 87.

Student B, turn to page 99.

3 Work in groups of three. Make suggestions for these situations. Spend five minutes on each situation. One person writes down the suggestions. Then share your ideas with the class.

- I need to get a birthday present for my dad, but I don't know what to get.
- I want to make some friends in other countries.
- I have a one-week holiday. I want to go somewhere interesting.

For example: *Why don't you go to Hawaii?*

Conversation strategy Sounding polite

Language can be polite or impolite, but your tone of voice – how you sound when you say something – is also very important.

1 1.23 Listen to these sentences said two different ways. The first way is polite; the second way is impolite.

Why don't you bring your own lunch?

You should talk to your manager.

2 1.24 Listen to the conversations. Pay attention to the speakers' tone of voice. Which responses sound polite? Which don't? Tick (✓) the appropriate box.

		polite	impolite
a	A: I don't know how to use this fax machine.		
	B: It's really easy.	☐	☐
b	A: I feel exhausted!		
	B: Why don't you sit down?	☐	☐
c	A: I don't have the company's phone number.		
	B: How about looking it up online?	☐	☐
d	A: How can I get to the restaurant?		
	B: How about taking a taxi?	☐	☐

3 Practise the conversations with a partner. Student B should first try to sound impolite. Practise again, and student B should try to sound polite. Take turns being A and B.

Viewpoints Corporate culture

1 Read what these employees from around the world say about the corporate culture in their companies.

Marcus Bodine,
Software Designer, US

I work for a software company. We work hard, with a lot of overtime, but we have fun, too – for example, on Fridays, we wear casual clothes, like jeans and a Hawaiian shirt. Sometimes my group goes out for pizza together. And we always have a big company picnic in the summer. People bring their families, and we play softball.

Alma Hansson,
Accounts Manager, Sweden

I started working last year for an IT company. It's easy for me to talk to my co-workers and my managers. My manager wants me to give my opinion. In Sweden, we don't talk about our families or hobbies at work. I don't usually talk about my job with my family. We don't mix our work lives and our personal lives.

Hassan Zouabi,
Civil Servant, Egypt

I work in a government office in Cairo. I greet everyone in my office each day. Respect, good manners, and relationships between people are important! I talk and socialise with my co-workers while I work. Our managers praise the workers often. This makes us want to work harder.

2 Discuss these questions with a group.

- Which company or companies seem similar to ones in your country? Which are different?
- Which work customs do you think you'd like? Are there any you wouldn't like?
- Imagine you work for a company that you like very much. Tell your group three things that make it a good company to work for.

In business Company survey

Scenario: You work for a global manufacturing company. Your group has been asked to do a survey to find out how satisfied people are with their working conditions. Interview other members of the class about what they like and don't like.

1 Complete the table with notes on your own likes and dislikes. Remember to say why you like or dislike something.

	Likes (why?)	Dislikes (why?)
Overseas Business Trips		
Meetings		
Presentations		
Writing Reports		
Visiting Customers		
Your own:		

2 Work in pairs or groups of three. Ask and answer questions about each other's likes and dislikes. For example:

Do you like going on overseas business trips?

Yes, I do. It's exciting to visit new places. / No, I don't. It's hard for me to speak English all the time.

Do you like visiting customers?

Yes, I do. I like meeting new people. / No, I don't. I get nervous.

3 With a different pair or group, talk about your likes and dislikes. Choose two areas and complete the following word webs with information you have collected.

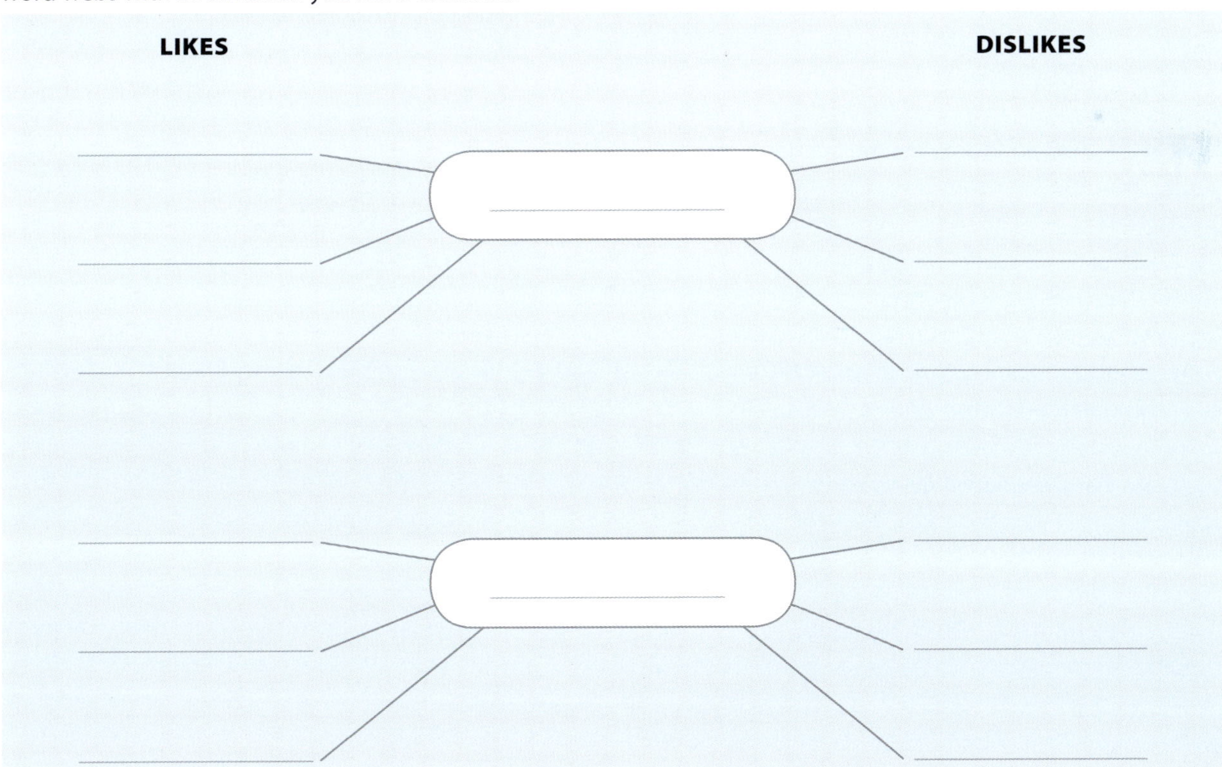

4 Share your word webs with other class members.

Review: Units 1–4

1 Sentence scramble

Unscramble the sentences. Then number them in the correct order to make a conversation. Then practise with a partner.

interesting wow Bangkok that's ! ____ ______________________________ !

office head in our Bangkok is . ____ ______________________________ .

company old is how the ? __1__ ______________________________ ?

where head office your is ? ____ ______________________________ ?

1956 were established we in . ____ ______________________________ .

2 Face-to-face

Use these cards to introduce yourself to a partner.

Start the conversation.

↓

Introduce yourself.

↓

Talk about your job (exchange cards).

↓

End the conversation.

3 Crossword

Look at the clues and complete the puzzle.

Across:

1 I can't do this puzzle. It's too d__________

3 I need to learn many new things in my job. It's c__________ but I enjoy it.

5 I don't mind studying English. Sometimes it's i__________

6 I can't stand housework. It's so b__________

Down:

2 I like this puzzle a lot. It's f__________

4 I enjoy visiting new places. It's e__________

4 Matching pairs

Connect A and B to make questions.

1 Can you	a do you work for?
2 Where	b Nissan build cars?
3 Why don't	c was Amazon established?
4 How do you	d about you?
5 Who	e repeat that?
6 How	f do you do?
7 When	g offices do you have?
8 How about	h you study harder?
9 Does	i like your job?
10 How many	j do you work?
11 What	k taking a rest?

5 Happy and sad

1.25

Listen to these five people. React (e.g. 'Wow!', 'Really?', 'I'm sorry to hear that') when you hear the beep.

6 Daily life

Complete the information for yourself. Describe your routine to a partner. When you listen, remember to reflect / react.

Every day Most days Some days	I	wake up at ________ . eat ________ for breakfast. ________ . ________ . ________ . go to sleep at ________ .

7 Which preposition?

Put the correct prepositions in the spaces.

I met my friend ________ 12 o' clock ________ Saturday. ________ 12:30 ________ three we went bowling. ________ the evening we went to karaoke. Next week ________ the 14th we are going hiking. ________ summer we are going on holiday to the USA together.

8 Company profile

Ask and answer questions about Natural Beauty with a partner. Then give an answer and ask someone to make the question.

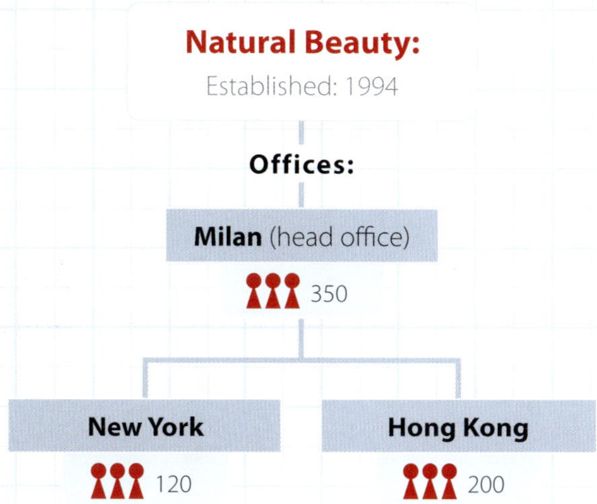

9 What's the matter?

1.26 Jill has many problems. Listen and make a suggestion when you hear the beep. You can use the ideas here or make your own. Remember to sound polite!

go to the bank
drink some water
take a rest
take some medicine
eat lunch
call the help desk

UNIT

5

Can I take a message?

Aims

- Talking on the phone
- Answering the phone
- Controlling language
- Taking a message
- Ending a call
- Viewpoints: Mobile phones
- In business: Receiving and passing on messages

Listen and practise Talking on the phone

1 Describe the photos. Where are they? What are they saying?

2 1.27 Listen to the telephone call. Write T for true or F for false next to each sentence. Then check your answers with a partner.

a Sam wants to speak to Vincent. ______ b Vincent is out of the office. ______

3 1.27 Listen again and complete the conversation. Then practise with a partner. Take turns being the receptionist and Sam.

Receptionist:	Prima Donna Fashions. How can I help you?
Sam:	Hello, can I ______ ______ Vincent Campbell please?
Receptionist:	Can I have ______ ______ please?
Sam:	It's Sam Montpellier from Fierce Fabrics.
Receptionist:	I'm sorry, I can't hear you. Can you repeat that?
Sam:	Yes, of course. It's Sam Montpellier from Fierce Fabrics.
Receptionist:	Thank you, Mr Montpellier. I'll transfer your call.
Vincent:	Hello, ______ ______ Vincent ______ .

4 Practise the conversation again. Change the names in blue using the information below.

Caller	Receptionist	Receiver
Mary Chan (Pacific Finance)	Tour Asia	Lek Phikul
Jeff Howes (C&F Stores)	Timson Watches	Ben Poole
Mike Burns (Golden Palace)	Snappy Snack Foods	Nancy Chen

5 1.28 What do you think Sam will say next? Tick (✓) your guesses. Then listen to see if you are correct.

a ☐ How are you?
b ☐ Vincent, can I meet you today?
c ☐ Vincent, this is Sam Montpellier. How are you?
d ☐ I'm calling to ask if we can meet today.

Answering the phone

1 Look at the table. It shows ways you can answer the phone.

Good	morning.	(Comet Technologies).	Can I help you?
	afternoon.		How can I help you?
	evening.		May I help you?

2 1.29 Listen and repeat what you hear. Use the same intonation.

a Good morning. Northwest Media Services … ?
b Good evening. Corporate Training Solutions … ?
c Good afternoon. Aztec Coffee … ?
d Good morning. Marco Supermarkets … ?

Conversation strategy Controlling language

1 Write the questions (a–e) next to the correct category to show different ways of controlling language. Check your answers with a partner.

a Can you speak more loudly?
b Can you repeat that?
c How do you spell (that)?
d Can you speak more slowly?
e Can you say that again?

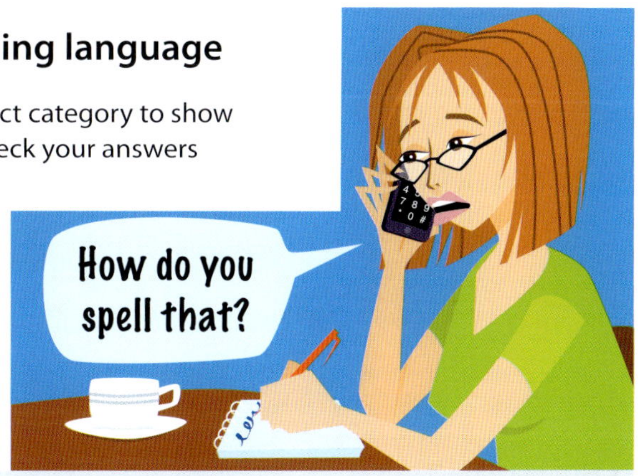

Controlling language

Speed ____________________

____________________ Volume

Repetition *Can you repeat that?*
____

____________________ Spelling

(**Note:** English speakers sometimes say *Speak louder* in informal situations.)

2 1.30 Listen to four conversations and write the letter (a–d) of the question you hear.

a ______ b ______ c ______ d ______

Taking a message

1 1.31 Listen to the conversation. Then practise with a partner.

Receptionist: Ashwell Transportation. How can I help you?

Caller: Can I speak to Kevin Aston, please? This is Tim Horowitz.

Receptionist: Just a moment, please. … Hello? I'm sorry, but Mr Aston is in a meeting. Can I take a message?

2 Practise the conversation with a different partner. Change the information in blue using your real names and the information below.

out of the office	on holiday	not at his desk
on a business trip	off sick	on another line

3 Look at the table. It shows phrases you can use for messages.

Can I take a message?	Yes.	Please ask her to call me back. Please tell her I called.
	No,	thank you. I'll call back later. that's OK. Thank you.

4 Practise with a partner. Use this conversation map.

Caller:	Receptionist:
'Ring, ring.'	Give company name.
Ask to speak to Ms …	Ask caller to repeat that. Ask caller to speak more slowly.
Repeat slowly.	Ask for caller's name.
Give name.	Ask caller to speak louder.
Give name again.	Ask caller to wait. Tell caller that Ms / Mr … is (*not there*). Offer to take a message.
Respond.	

5 1.32 Listen and complete the messages below.

a

2:40
Tom,
Margaret ____________ from ____________
Corporation called. Can you call her
back after ____________ ?
Her number is 090 – ____________ –
____________ .
Hisako.

b

Josh Brown

Date: 22nd March Time: 09:30

Message: José ____________ from the
Philippines called.
He will call you back ____________ .

Taken by: Maria

c

While you were out:

Caller: Manuel ____________
of Aztec Coffee

Tel: ____________

Please call back | No message
Will call you back | Other

Message:

Received by: Heena TIme: 10:25

d

From: Alison Chen
To: Peter Weybridge
Subject: <Important> Telephone Call

Peter,

Ms. ____________ from ____________ called this morning.
Can you call her back as soon as possible?

Her number is 01 ________ 87 ________

Regards,
Alison

Ending a call

1 Look at these ways of ending a phone call.

Receiver	Caller
a I'll give (her) your message. b Thank you for calling. c Thank you for your call. d Goodbye.	e Thank you. f Goodbye.

2 1.32 Listen again to the conversations in exercise 5. Which phrases do they use to end the calls? Write the letters in the boxes for each conversation.

a ☐ ☐ ☐ ☐   c ☐ ☐ ☐ ☐
b ☐ ☐ ☐ ☐   d ☐ ☐ ☐ ☐

Talk business

Student A, turn to page 88.

Student B, turn to page 100.

Viewpoints Mobile phones

1 Answer these questions for yourself. Compare your answers with other class members.

- Do you have a mobile phone?
- What do people in your country use mobile phones for?

2 1.33 Listen to people from three different countries talking about their mobile phones. Tick (✓) the sentences you hear.

Hye-won Park, Sales Clerk, Korea

- ☐ I send 20 to 30 text messages a day.
- ☐ I don't use it at the office.
- ☐ I can use my phone as a train pass.
- ☐ It's not convenient.

Melissa Golding, Student, US

- ☐ My parents call me every week.
- ☐ I don't text much – it's easier and cheaper to email.
- ☐ I feel safe if I'm driving.
- ☐ I hate it when people use their phones in restaurants.

Thomas Müeller, Engineer, Germany

- ☐ The company uses it to contact me.
- ☐ I like to play games.
- ☐ I also read the news on the internet.
- ☐ I use the alarm when I stay in hotels.

3 Discuss these questions in a small group.

- Which person is most like you (or people from your country)?
- Are there any rules in your country about where you cannot use mobile phones?
- Do people in your country use mobile phones on buses and trains? In restaurants?

4 What functions are important to you when you buy or use a mobile phone? Rate these items 1–5 (1 = very important, 5 = not important). Talk about your answers in a group.

Colour	
Size	
Cost	
Alarm	
(Your idea)	

Camera	
Internet	
TV	
Calculator	

Music	
Games	
Text messages	
Schedule	

In business Receiving and passing on messages

Scenario: You work in a sales office with two colleagues. Both of your colleagues are away from the office. You will need to take messages for them while they are away. You also need to call two customers. If the customers are not there, leave a message.

1 In the space below, write down your name, your company name, and your telephone number.

Name:	
Company Name:	
Tel:	

2 On a piece of paper, write down the names of your two colleagues so the rest of your class can see them.

3 Work in groups of four. With different partners, make and receive two phone calls. Use the forms below to write down the messages you receive.

Message for:

Caller:

Company:

Tel:

☐ Please call back
☐ Will call you back
☐ No message
☐ Other

Message:

Received by: Time:

Message for:

Caller:

Company:

Tel:

☐ Please call back
☐ Will call you back
☐ No message
☐ Other

Message:

Received by: Time:

4 After you have made and received your calls, check with your partners that the information in the messages is correct.

UNIT 6

Which ones should we order?

Aims

- Discussing products
- Describing and comparing products
- Understanding advertisements
- Softening language
- Viewpoints: Advertising
- In business: Advertise your company

material: ______ % cotton
______ % polyester
country: Spain
No. of colours: ____________

material: ______ % bamboo
______ % cotton
country: ____________
No. of colours: ____________

Listen and practise Discussing products

1 Describe the photos. What do they show?

2 1.34 Juan is giving a presentation to the Purchasing Department. Listen and tick (✓) which T-shirts he prefers.

☐ Costa del Cool
☐ Trip Tees

3 1.34 Listen again and complete the brochures with the correct information. Check your answers with a partner.

4 1.35 How else will Juan compare the two companies? What will he talk about? Tick (✓) your guesses. Then listen to see if you are correct.

a ☐ price b ☐ size c ☐ quality d ☐ style

Describing and comparing products

1 Look at the table. It shows words you can use to describe products. Complete the table with a partner. Can you think of any more words?

	-er / -ier	**more - (than)**
cheap	cheaper	
compact		more compact
easy	easier	
energy-efficient		
fast		
heavy		
light		
new		
reliable		

2 Look at the table again and talk with a partner. When do you add *-er* to a word? *-ier*? When do you use *more*? Note these exceptions:

good - better
bad - worse
fun - more fun

3 Read the conversation with a partner.

A: This looks like a great camera. And it's really cheap.
B: Yeah. But I think that one is cheaper. It's also more compact.
A: Hmm. You're right. That's important.

4 Practise the conversation again. Change the products and the descriptions in blue using the ideas below.

a **camera**
light; compact

b **software package**
fast; new

c **mobile phone**
energy-efficient; easy to use

d **video game**
fun; challenging

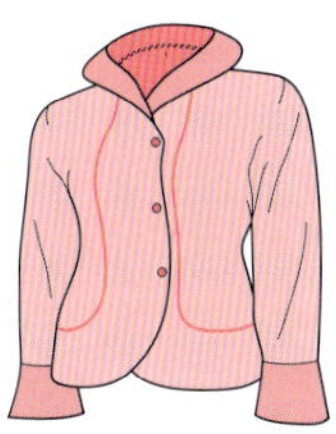

e **jacket**
attractive; cheap

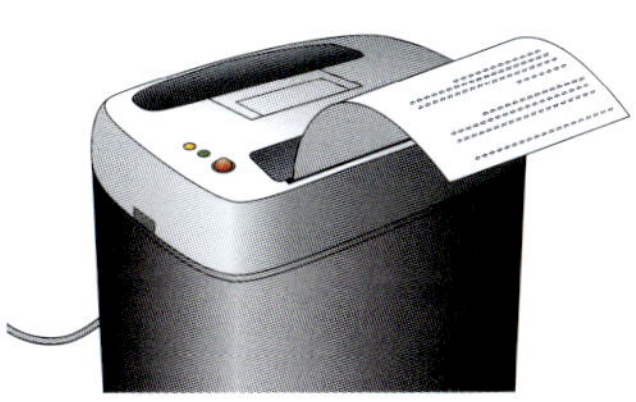

f **shredder**
compact; reliable

g **sandwich**
cheap; delicious

h **scooter**
reliable; energy-efficient

Understanding advertisements

1 Match the words and phrases with their definitions.

a buy one, get one free __3__
b coupon ______
c a 10% discount; 10% off ______
d free shipping ______
e money-back guarantee ______
f on sale ______

1 When you order something, you only pay for the item. You don't pay any mailing costs.
2 A product costs 10% less than it usually does.
3 If you buy one product, you get another one without paying any more money.
4 If you don't like the product, you can return it and the shop will return your money.
5 A product costs less money than it usually does.
6 A piece of paper that promises you can pay less money or get some money back (a refund).

2 1.36 Listen and complete the advertisements.

a

Do you need to get in ______ before the summer? Come to Gym of the Stars!

Home | Classes | Times | Gym | Facilities

______ with our top fitness instructors! Daily dance and martial arts ______ help you lose weight and look your ______ – and have ______!

All of our classes have a ______ ______ ______.

If you're not happy, we'll give you a full ______!

Special! This week only, check online and in your local paper for valuable ______! Use them to get a ______ on our diet drinks and vitamins.

Or order online and receive ______ shipping.

b

Total Fitness

When you're ______ about your health, you're ready for Total Fitness!

Work with a fitness instructor to get ______ results. You'll look and ______ better.

Sign up with a friend, and you'll each get ______ off the first month's fee.

Pay for a one-year membership and get ______!

Talk business

Student A, turn to page 89.
Student B, turn to page 101.

Conversation strategy Softening language

1 1.37 Listen to the two conversations between a Sales Assistant and a customer. Which one is more polite? Why?

Conversation 1

A: How do you like this printer?
B: Well, it's kind of large, don't you think?
A: Hmmm. But it's easy to use.
B: I don't know. It's also not very energy-efficient.

Conversation 2

A: How do you like this watch?
B: It's too small.
A: Hmmm. But it's attractive.
B: It's also not cheap.

2 Practise Conversation 1 with a partner. Underline the phrases in the first conversation that soften the expression, to make it less direct. Add those phrases to Conversation 2. Then practise with a partner.

3 Look at the table. It shows ways that you can soften your language.

Instead of *too*	Instead of *not*	At the beginning of a sentence		At the end of a sentence
a bit kind of rather	not very not really not so	Well… Actually…	To be honest… I don't know.	…don't you think?

4 1.38 Listen to these conversations comparing products. Write down the softening language they use.

a ______________________________

b ______________________________

5 Talk about these products with a partner.

expensive, fast, energy-efficient

small, cheap, difficult-to-use

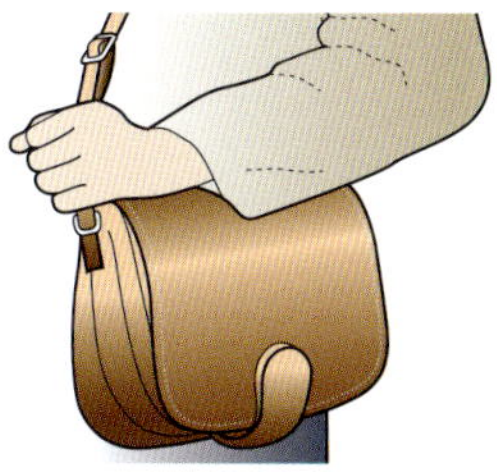

expensive, fashionable, practical

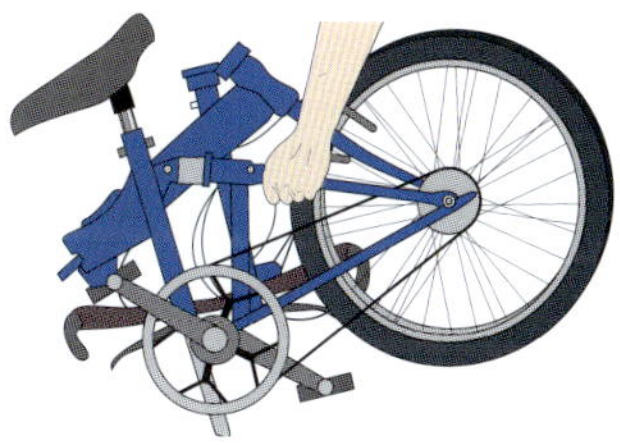

heavy, compact, expensive

Viewpoints Advertising

1 Read what these people from around the world say about advertisements.

Helen Curtis,
Nurse, UK

I'm annoyed by most ads. I don't like ads interrupting radio or TV programmes. That's why I mostly watch the BBC, which doesn't have any ads. These days, magazines seem to be mostly ads! Even some articles are really just trying to sell you a product. I'm especially annoyed by internet ads. When I'm trying to read a website, I don't like large flashing ads for some product I'm not interested in.

Ayako Awano,
Designer, Japan

Actually, I like a lot of TV ads. In Japan, companies never compare themselves directly to another company or criticise their competitors. So the ads focus on giving you a good impression of the product and the company. Many ads on TV today are funny or clever. They use a lot of attractive images, popular music, and celebrities. In fact, sometimes the ads are better than the programmes!

Henri Latour,
Student, France

I don't pay much attention to TV ads, so they don't bother me. I'm not impressed by celebrity endorsements, though – I don't believe a car is better because someone famous drives it. I look at internet ads sometimes. It's a good way to find special offers, coupons, and discounts. I don't mind ads if they save me money.

2 Discuss these questions in a group.

- Which person is most like you?
- What kinds of ads annoy you? What kinds of ads do you like?
- How often do you see ads? Where do you see them?
- What do you think about celebrity endorsements? What famous people advertise products that you know about? Have you ever bought any of those products?

In business Advertise your company

Scenario: Your group have been asked to create some advertising for a company. Create an advert that will encourage people to buy their products or use their services.

1 Discuss in your group. Make notes.

- What product or service you are advertising. What is it called?
- Where the advert is going to appear (TV, magazine, radio, web, etc.)
- What words you are going to use to describe the product or service.
- If you are going to include any special offers (discounts, coupons, etc.)
- If you are going to use other ideas (celebrity endorsements, comparisons with other products, surveys, etc.)

2 Write a slogan for your product or service. A slogan is a short sentence or phrase that helps a product or service to sell.

Think of some examples of products and their slogans that you know in your group.

Write your own slogan for your product as a group.

3 Plan the advert here. Either write the script, or design the advert.

4 Describe your ideas to the class.

UNIT 7

Are you free on Tuesday?

Aims

- Making arrangements
- Making a telephone call
- Checking information
- Making an appointment
- Viewpoints: Using technology to communicate
- In business: Make an appointment

Listen and practise Making arrangements

1 Describe the photos. Where are they? What are they doing?

2 1.39 Listen to the telephone call. Write T for true or F for false next to each sentence. Then check your answers with a partner.

a Carolyn wants to meet Amanda next week. ______

b Amanda is busy on Tuesday afternoon. ______

3 1.39 Listen again and complete the conversation. Then practise with a partner. Take turns being Carolyn and Amanda.

Carolyn: Hi Amanda, this is Carolyn. How are you?

Amanda: Hi Carolyn! I'm fine, thanks. How are you?

Carolyn: Very well, thank you. ______ ______ ______ ask if we can meet this week.

Amanda: Certainly. ______ ______ ______ my diary. When is good for you?

Carolyn: ______ ______ ______ on Tuesday at ten?

Amanda: Let me see. No, sorry. ______ ______ ______ . I'm free in the afternoon. How about half past two?

Carolyn: Half past two is fine.

4 Practise the conversation again. Change the information in blue using your real names and the times below.

Caller 	Receiver 	
on Wednesday at three	in the morning	eleven
on the 25th	on the 26th	four o'clock
tomorrow at nine	on Tuesday	half past nine
Friday evening	in the afternoon	half past three

5 1.40 What do you think Carolyn will say next? Tick (✓) your guesses. Then listen to see if you are correct.

a ☐ She will ask where they will meet.
b ☐ She will repeat the day and time.
c ☐ She will tell Amanda why she wants to meet.
d ☐ She will ask Amanda for her email address.

Making a telephone call

1 Look at the table. It shows ways you can begin a telephone call.

<table>
<tr><td rowspan="6">Hello, …
Hello, this is …
Hello, my name is …</td><td>Can I speak to</td><td colspan="2">Mr / Ms ………………… , please?
the Sales Manager, please?
room service, please?</td></tr>
<tr><td>I'm calling to
I'd like to</td><td>change
confirm
order</td><td>(my reservation).
(our meeting time).
(some flowers).</td></tr>
<tr><td rowspan="3">I'm calling about</td><td colspan="2">(our meeting tomorrow).</td></tr>
<tr><td colspan="2">(your email).</td></tr>
<tr><td colspan="2">(my reservation).</td></tr>
<tr><td colspan="3">I'm returning your call.</td></tr>
</table>

2 1.41 Listen and connect the receiver with the caller and the purpose / subject.

Receiver 	**Caller** 	**Purpose / Subject**
a Toni's Pizza	Mario Fera	Make a reservation
b Jaidev Singh	Junji Tanaka	Meeting time
c Westwood Hotel	Josh Brown	Order food
d José Reina	Rachel Carson	Returning a call

3 Practise making calls with a partner using the information below. Take turns being the receiver and the caller.

Receiver	**Caller**
a Grand Hotel Receptionist	Call the Grand Hotel to change your reservation.
b Bill Smith	Call Bill Smith to change your meeting time.
c Maria Vega	Call Maria Vega to return her call.
d Sunset Holidays	Call Sunset Holidays to confirm your reservation.

Conversation strategy Checking information

1 Look at the table. It shows ways you can check information or confirm that you understand what someone has said.

Let me confirm. Let me repeat that.	Your number is … You said … You want to change … Thursday at six o'clock.	Is that right?

2 1.42 Listen to the call. Follow this conversation map.

Caller:	Receptionist:
'Ring, ring.'	Give the company name. Offer to help.
Ask to speak to …	Ask for the caller's name.
Give your name.	Ask the caller to spell his / her family name.
Spell your family name.	Ask the caller to wait. Tell the caller that Ms / Mr … is (*out of the office*). Offer to take a message.
Ask him / her to call you back.	Ask the caller for their telephone number.
Give the telephone number.	Ask the caller to speak more slowly.
Repeat the telephone number.	Check the information (*telephone number*).
Agree.	Check the information (*name, number, message*).
Agree.	End the call.
End the call.	

3 Practise with a partner using the conversation map in exercise 2. Use your own ideas for company, names, number, and message. Use the chart to make notes.

Company: ______________________

Name: ______________________

Number: ______________________

Message: ______________________

____

____

____

Talk business

Student A, turn to page 90.

Student B, turn to page 102.

Making an appointment

1 Look at the tables. They show phrases you can use to make appointments.

Question		→	Answer	
When are you free? When is good for you? What time is good for you?		→	I'm free	(on Tuesday). (at 11:30).
Are you free	(on Monday)? (at two o'clock)? (on the 25th)?	→	Sorry,	I'm busy then.
			Yes,	I'm free then.
How about	(Monday)? (five o'clock)?	→	That's fine. Five o'clock is fine.	

2 1.43 Listen to these conversations. Where and when will they meet? Check your answers with a partner.

Conversation 1

Day:

Time:

Place:

Conversation 2

Day:

Time:

Place:

Conversation 3

Day:

Time:

Place:

3 Practise with a partner using your own names. Follow this conversation map.

Caller:

- 'Ring, ring.'
- Give your name. Ask how he / she is.
- Reply. Say you are calling to ask if he / she is free for a meeting.
- Ask if he / she is free on (day).
- Say that is fine. Ask if he / she is free at (time).
- Confirm day and time.
- End the call.

Receiver:

- Give your name. Offer to help.
- Reply and reflect (*And you?*).
- Say you will check your schedule. Ask when is good for him / her.
- Say you are busy then. Give another day.
- Agree.
- Agree.
- End the call.

Viewpoints Using technology to communicate

1 1.44 Listen to people from three different countries talking about how they communicate. Make notes as you listen.

Silvia Rossi, Project Manager, Italy

Email:
Voicemail:
Telephone:
Teleconference:
Meetings:

Tran Chung Nguyen, Assistant Sales Manager, Vietnam

Email:
Voicemail:
Telephone:
Teleconference:
Meetings:

Masako Mori, HR Officer, Japan

Email:
Voicemail:
Telephone:
Teleconference:
Meetings:

2 Tick (✓) the boxes with your own information.

	Use	**Don't use**	**Like**	**Don't like**
Email				
Telephone				
Teleconference				
Face-to-face				
Text messages				
Chat				

3 Talk about your answers in a small group. Use some of this vocabulary.

complicated efficient formal inefficient informal quick simple slow

For example:

A: *Do you use email?*
B: *Yes, I do. / No, I don't. How about you?*
A: *I like email because it's quick. What do you think?*
C: *Me too. I don't like chat because it's informal. How about you?*

In business Make an appointment

Scenario: You are new to a company and want to arrange short meetings with people from other departments in the company. You must arrange at least six meetings.

1 Complete the schedule with at least three or four things you have to do this week (meetings, business trips, studying, lunch appointments, etc.) and schedule times for them.

	MONDAY	TUESDAY	WEDNESDAY	THURSDAY	FRIDAY
9:00		Visit			
10:00		Customer			
11:00				Meeting	
12:00	Lunch			Lunch	
1:00					
2:00					
3:00					
4:00					
5:00					
6:00			Teleconference		

2 Workwith a partner, make a phone call and decide on a time to meet that is convenient for you both and write down their name and their department in the correct place.

3 Change partners and make a new phone call until you have at least six appointments made with members of your class.

UNIT 8

Where's the Marketing Department?

Aims

- Getting directions
- Prepositions of place
- Giving a tour
- Viewpoints: Workplace facilities
- In business: Give a company tour

Listen and practise Getting directions

1 Describe the photos. Where are they? What are they saying?

2 1.45 Listen to the conversation. Circle the correct answer.

a Brett is at *his / someone else's* company.

b Brett *knows / doesn't know* where to go.

3 1.45 Listen again and complete the conversation. Then practise with a partner. Take turns being the receptionist and Brett.

Receptionist: Can I ____________ you?

Brett: Yes. I'm Brett Silvermann, and I have a 3:00 appointment with Jack McAvoy in Marketing.

Receptionist: OK, Mr Silvermann, you can go ____________ up.

Brett: Thanks. Uh… how do I ____________ ____________ the Marketing Department?

Receptionist: Oh, it's on the third floor. When you ____________ out of the lift, turn right and ____________ ____________ the hall. It's the second door on your left, and it says "Marketing Department" on it. You can't ____________ it.

Brett: Thanks. Oh, and, uh, ____________ the lift?

4 Practise the conversation again. Change the information in blue using the times and places below.

Brett	10:30am meeting lunch appointment 2:00pm appointment	Production Sales Accounting

Receptionist	seventh second fourth	turn right go straight turn left	the first room after the stairs the last room on your right just after the drinking fountain	Production Sales Accounting

5 1.46 What do you think the receptionist will do next? Tick (✓) your guesses. Then listen to see if you are correct.

a ☐ She will tell Brett where the lift is.
b ☐ She will draw a map.
c ☐ She will call Mr McAvoy in Marketing.
d ☐ She will take Brett to the third floor.

Prepositions of place

1 Where is the desk? Label each picture with words and phrases from the box.

across from	between	in the corner	next to / on the right
behind	in front of	next to / on the left	under

a ______________

b ______________

c ______________

d ______________

e ______________

f ______________

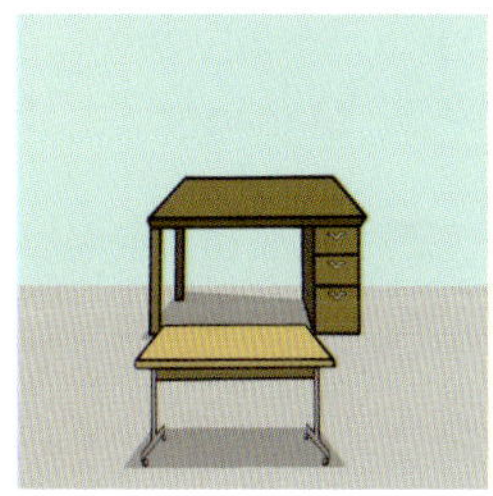

g ______________

h ______________

2 1.47 Listen to two people talking about an office. Label the desks that belong to these people. Write the correct letter on the desk.

a the boss b the personal assistant c Ken d Sophie

3 Look at the office on page 51. Practise with a partner asking and answering questions about the picture.

For example: A: *Excuse me. Where's the fax machine?*
B: *Oh, it's over there, next to Sophie's desk, on the right.*

Now ask and answer questions about these things:

a coffee maker b plant c water cooler d exit

Giving a tour

1 1.48 Listen to a hotel manager showing the hotel to a new front desk receptionist. Practise the conversation with a partner. Take turns being the manager and the receptionist.

Manager: Come with me, please. OK, this is the lobby, of course. There's a cash machine in the corner there. Oh, and a public phone, next to the cash machine. Any questions?

Receptionist: Yes, is the lobby open 24 hours?

Manager: Yes, it is. Now, let's go to the lifts. They're next to the stairs. This lift on the left goes only to the rooms. It doesn't stop on the first, second, or third floors. And this one here, this one stops on every floor. We'll go to the first floor to begin – that's the dining room and the lounge – and then to the second floor, the business centre. Um, any questions so far?

Receptionist: What's on the third floor?

Manager: The swimming pool and the fitness centre. OK, come with me.

2 Look at the table. It shows directions and questions you can use when you talk to groups of people.

Directions	Questions
Come with me, please. Follow me.	Any questions? Is that clear? Are you with me so far?
Listen carefully. Watch closely.	Can everyone hear me? Can everyone see?
Let's go now. Let's stop here.	Is everyone with me?

Talk business

Student A, turn to page 91.
Student B, turn to page 103.

3 1.49 Listen to these group tours. Tick (✓) the question that you hear. Then write the response.

a ☐ Are you with me so far?
☐ Is everyone with me? *No, Sandy's at the drinking fountain.*

b ☐ Can everyone see?
☐ Any questions? ______

c ☐ OK? Is that clear?
☐ OK? Can you hear? ______

d ☐ Is everyone here?
☐ Can everyone hear me? ______

4 Work in groups of 3–5. One of you is the HR Manager of a factory. The others are new employees. Take turns being the manager and give the new employees a tour. Use the map below. Start at the "X."

Begin like this:

OK, follow me, please. Let's go straight down this path. On the left is the research laboratory. …

Viewpoints Workplace facilities

1 Read what these people say about their workplaces.

Rodrigo de Santos, Marketing Executive, Brazil

I work for a small marketing company. At the office, we only have a small cafeteria and some vending machines. But my company gives us discounts at many local businesses, including restaurants, shops, health clinics, hotels, and a health club.

Young-kwang Oh, Factory Worker, Korea

I work in a factory. Because we often work overtime, and because there are a lot of different shifts, workers don't always have time to go shopping during the week. So we have a small convenience store on site, and also a cash machine, a chemist, a hairdresser's, and a laundry service.

Lise Martin, Clerk, Canada

I work for an insurance company. Ten years ago, we had on-site daycare. But the company found out that working parents preferred a flexible schedule. Now we have facilities like a cafeteria, a gym, and a locker room. There's also a yoga class that meets twice a week during the lunch hour.

2 Imagine you are working at a medium-sized company five years from now. How important would these facilities be to you? Tick (✓) the appropriate column.

	Very important / necessary	**Not necessary, but attractive**	**Not interesting or useful to me**
on-site daycare			
a gym			
a cafeteria			
a convenience store			
a bank or a cash machine			
a chemist			
a hairdresser's			
showers			
a travel agency			

3 Talk about your answers in a small group, and discuss these questions.

a What other facilities would you like your company to have?

b Do you think your answers would be different 10 or 15 years from now?

In business Giving a company tour

Scenario: You have been asked to arrange a tour of your company for some new employees who are starting work soon. First write an email inviting them on the tour, then arrange the tour.

1 Read the invitation email. Complete the gaps so that the invitation comes from you.

Dear ______________

I would like to invite you to a tour of the company on ______________,
at ______________.

We will be meeting in ______________ which is down the hall from the cafeteria, the third door on the left.

Please let me know if you can attend this tour as soon as possible.

I look forward to hearing from you soon.

All the best,

____

2 Work with a partner. Choose one of the following types of company (or use your own idea).

Bank	Clothing Company (Head Office)
Bicycle manufacturer	Research Laboratory (Pharmaceuticals)
Sports Club	Your own idea:

3 With your partner, write a list of the most important facilities your company has that new employees will need to know about.

4 Draw a map or floor plan of your company. Include the facilities you would want to show the new employees.

5 Work in a small group. Take it in turns to show the others your map and guide them around your company.

Review: Units 5–8

1 Be polite

Change the conversation to make it more polite. Then practise with a partner.

Receptionist:	BL Chemicals.
Kevin:	I want Jon Philpott.
Receptionist:	What's your name?
Kevin:	Kevin Aston, Ashwell Transportation.
Receptionist:	Can't hear. Say it louder.
Kevin:	Kevin Aston. Ashwell Transportation.
Receptionist:	Spell your family name.
Kevin:	A-S-T-O-N.
Receptionist:	Wait.

2 Controlling language

What can you say if …

someone speaks too quietly?

someone speaks too quickly?

you want someone to repeat something?

you want someone to spell something?

3 Conversation map

Use this map to have a telephone conversation with a partner.

Caller:	**Receptionist:**
'Ring, ring.' →	Give company name. Offer to help.
← Ask to speak to Ms … →	Ask for caller's name.
← Give name. →	Ask caller to repeat it.
← Give name again. →	Ask caller to wait. Tell caller that Ms / Mr … is (*not there*). Offer to take message.
← Respond.	

4 Word square

Hidden in the square are 12 adjectives to describe products. How many words can you find in five minutes? (Look in these directions: ↓ →)

g	e	o	i	s	t	e	n	d	f	r	a
a	w	r	e	l	i	a	b	l	e	q	c
i	d	a	s	e	p	s	l	i	t	u	o
b	s	t	m	e	r	y	x	g	t	f	m
t	t	x	a	y	r	r	n	h	i	s	p
e	r	n	l	i	w	s	j	t	u	t	a
a	o	d	l	e	t	t	i	k	v	i	c
a	n	u	e	f	f	i	c	i	e	n	t
r	g	o	w	f	t	s	e	v	l	o	d
t	z	k	s	s	b	u	f	l	a	s	p
e	h	e	a	v	y	r	a	v	i	c	e
n	o	f	f	l	i	k	s	c	o	h	e
m	a	t	t	r	a	c	t	i	v	e	g
u	r	d	l	u	s	h	a	n	e	a	t
d	e	l	i	c	i	o	u	s	i	p	s

5 What's the difference?

Use the adjectives in exercise 4 to compare the products. Which do you like better? Why?

6 *to* or *about*?

Complete the expressions with *to* or *about*. Then read them out loud with a partner.

I'm calling…

a ________ confirm my reservation.

b ________ my visit tomorrow.

c ________ change our meeting time.

d ________ your order #43256.

e ________ our appointment this afternoon.

f ________ ask if we can meet.

g ________ request some information.

h ________ lunch today.

7 Are you free on Monday?

Practise with a partner. Use this conversation map and use your own names.

Caller:	Receiver:
'Ring, ring.' →	Give your name.
Give your name. Ask how he / she is. →	Reply.
Reply. Say you are calling to ask if he / she is free for a meeting. →	Ask him / her to speak louder.
Repeat (louder).	

8 Where's the bank?

Add these places to the map:

bank cinema chemist post office

Then take turns giving a tour to other people.

UNIT 9

How long does the process take?

Aims

- Describing a process: sequencing
- Ordering a product
- Checking and confirming
- Recruiting
- Viewpoints: Looking for a job
- In business: Design a process

STEP 1

STEP 3

STEP 2

Listen and practise Sequencing

1 Describe the photos. What is happening? What are they doing?

2 1.50 Helen is describing a web design process to Sven and Jin Soo. Listen and write T for true or F for false next to each sentence.

a The first step is planning the design. ______

b The final step is to launch the web page. ______

3 1.50 Listen again and complete the conversation. Then practise with two partners. Take turns being Sven, Jin Soo, and Helen.

Helen: ______ ______ talk to the customers or users of the web page. This is the most important step, to find out what the customer needs. ______ ______, we plan the basic design of the web page. ______ ______ layout of text, graphics, and languages.

Sven: I see. And what do you do next?

Helen: The ______ ______ is we pilot the web page and get feedback from customers.

Jin Soo: Yes, customer feedback is very important.

Helen: ______ we get feedback we revise the design and make any changes or improvements. ______ ______ launch the new web page. Are there any questions?

4 1.51 What questions do you think Sven and Jin Soo will ask? Tick (✓) your guesses. Then listen to see if you are correct.

a ☐ How long does the process take?
b ☐ What colour is the web page?
c ☐ Who are the customers?
d ☐ How much does it cost?

Describing a process Sequencing

1 Look at the table. It shows ways you can describe the steps in a process.

First Second Third Fourth ………	After (that)… Before… Next… Then… At the same time… Finally…
The (first) step is…	

2 Look at these flow charts. Practise with a partner. Take turns describing the processes.

Begin like this: *There are ___ steps in this process. First you…*

a) A cup of tea

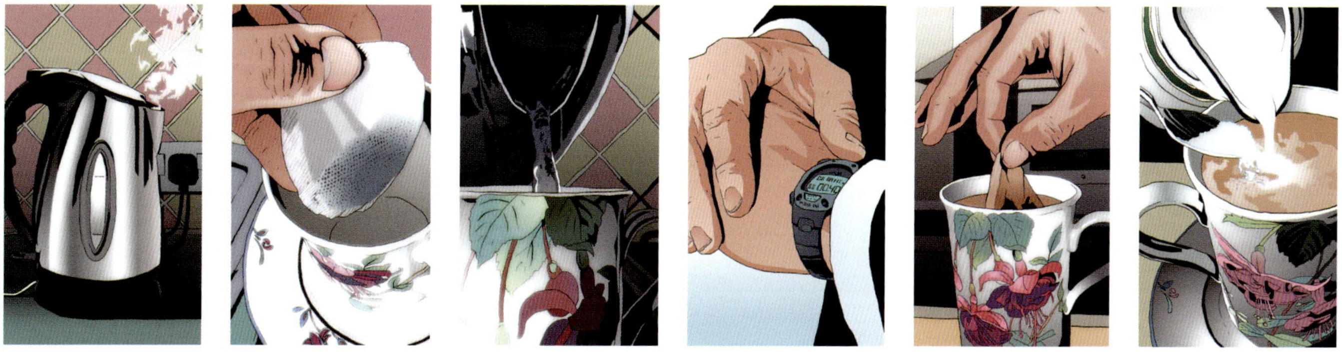

Heat the water. → Put a tea bag in the cup. → Pour boiling water into the cup. → Wait for 3–4 minutes. → Take out the tea bag. → Add milk and sugar if needed.

b) A mango smoothie

Peel and chop the fruit. → Add the fruit to the blender. → Add ice cubes and some yogurt. → Blend for about 1 minute. → Pour the smoothie into glasses.

Describing a process Ordering a product

1 Write these sentences under the illustrations.

> We send an invoice. We enter the data. We order the product from the factory.
> We check the inventory. We arrange delivery. We receive the order.

2 1.52 Then listen to Ella and check your answers.

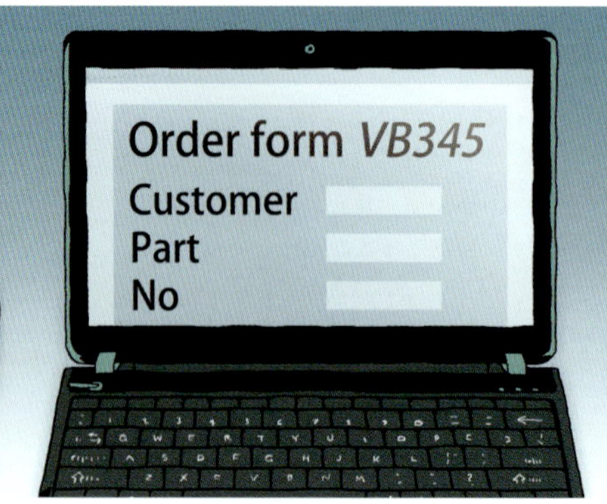

1 ______ 2 ______ 3 ______

4 ______ 5 ______ 6 ______

3 With a partner, use the sentences in exercise 1 to order the steps in the flow chart.

Customer order process

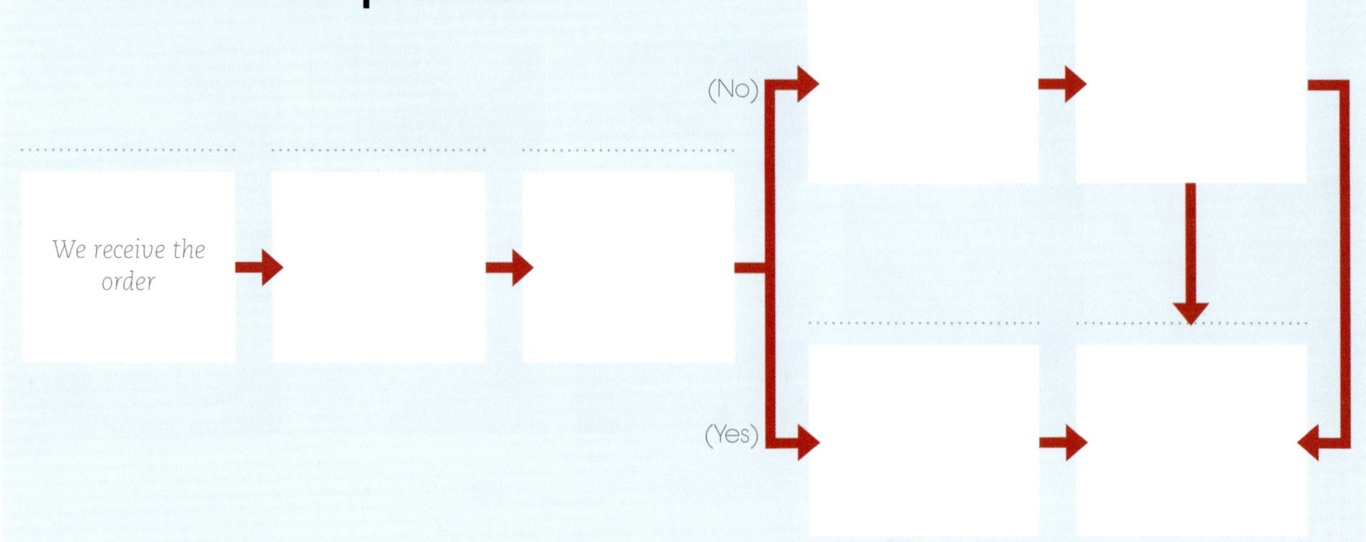

4 1.52 Listen again. Next to each step write down the sequencing language Ella uses.

5 Now describe the process to a partner. You can use the same language as Ella or you can change some of the language.

Conversation strategy review Checking and confirming

1 Look at the tables. They show ways you can check and confirm understanding.

Is that clear (so far)? Are you with me (so far)? OK?	Yes, that's clear. I understand / I'm with you. OK.
	Let me confirm that, … Let me repeat that, …

2 Choose one of the following and describe it to a partner. Remember to check and confirm the information.

How to use a mobile phone camera
How to make a photocopy
How to boil an egg
How to shampoo and condition your hair
How to brush your teeth
(your idea)

Describing a process Recruiting

Work in a group. Using these steps, describe a recruiting process. Choose one option from Steps 1, 2, and 3.

Begin like this: *There are four steps in our recruiting process. First we …*

STEP 1	Advertise online	Visit universities	Advertise in newspapers
STEP 2	Receive CVs by mail	Receive CVs online	
STEP 3	Give one-on-one interviews	Give group interviews	Give a written test
STEP 4	Choose the best employee!		

Talk business

Student A, turn to page 92.
Student B, turn to page 104.

Viewpoints Looking for a job

1 1.53 Listen to people from three countries talking about how they looked for a job. Match the person with what they say.

☐ It takes about a year!

☐ I talked to my professor and he recommended an internship.

☐ I went to 15 or 20 interviews.

a Junko Saito,
Designer, Japan

b Jean Durand,
Engineer, France

c Susan Russell,
Manager Trainee, US

☐ I looked on the internet.

☐ After I graduated the company offered me a job.

☐ You can't get experience without a job!

2 1.53 Now listen again and tick (✓) what method each person used to look for a job.

	Junko	Jean	Susan
Attended job fair			
Visited university job centre			
Friend's advice / recommendation			
Newspaper advertisement			
Professor's advice / recommendation			
Internet / website			

3 How do people in your country look for jobs after college or university? Talk about your answers in a small group.

In business Design a process

Scenario: Your company would like to improve efficiency by making a clear process that everyone will follow. Map it out with your team and present it to the group.

1 Choose from these following ideas the process you are going to design.

- How products are ordered
- How new product is developed
- How new employees are recruited
- Your own idea ____________________

2 Map out the process below in groups or pairs.

Process: ____________________

3 Work with a new partner or group. Describe your process and check/confirm understanding. After you have finished, repeat the exercise with another partner or group.

UNIT

10

Exports increased sharply

Aims

- Talking about data
- Talking about graphs
- Giving a presentation
- Answering questions
- Viewpoints: Presentations
- In business: Give a presentation

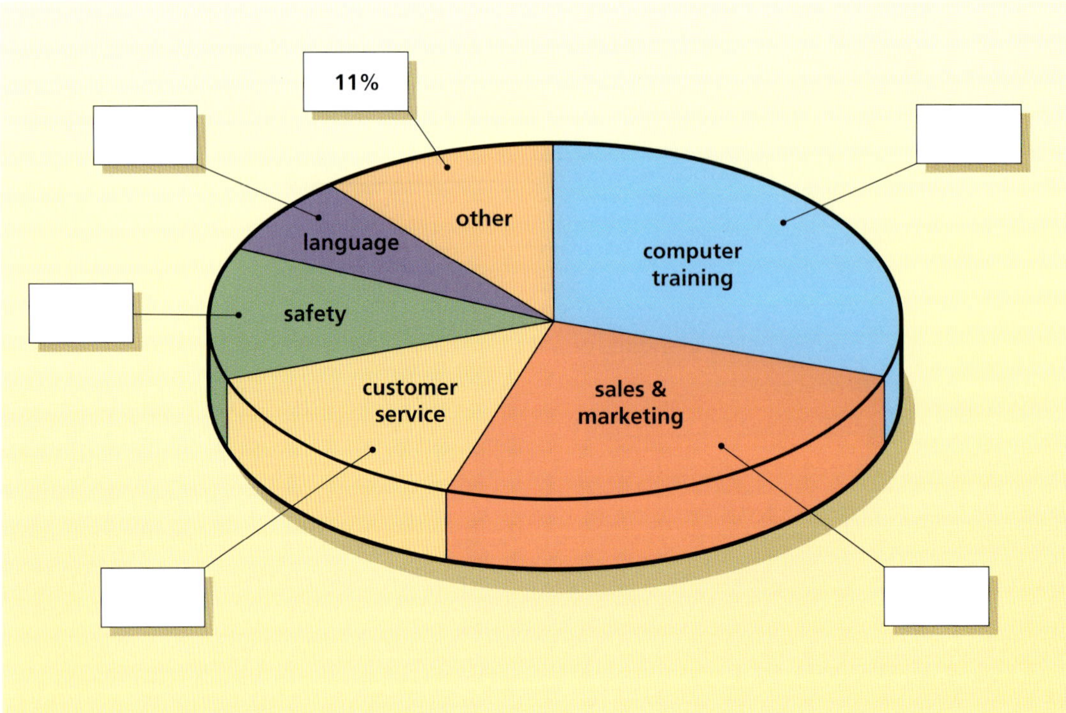

Listen and practise Talking about data

1 Look at the pie chart. What does it show?

2 2.01 Listen to Eduardo's presentation to the Marketing Department. What is the presentation about? Circle the correct answer.

a How to use the new computer system.

b How to spend money for training.

c Why language training is too expensive.

3 2.01 Listen again and complete the pie chart with the correct numbers.

4 Practise with a partner. Change the information in blue using the ideas in the pie chart. Take turns explaining the pie chart.

They spent 35 percent of the training budget on computers.

5 2.02 What do you think Eduardo will do next? Tick (✓) your guesses. Then listen to see if you are correct.

a ☐ He will suggest that everyone take a break.

b ☐ He will talk about next year's training needs.

c ☐ He will talk about how much money the company has now.

d ☐ He will check to see if anyone has any questions.

Talking about graphs

1 Look at the bar graph. What does it show? Why do you think the information is presented in a graph?

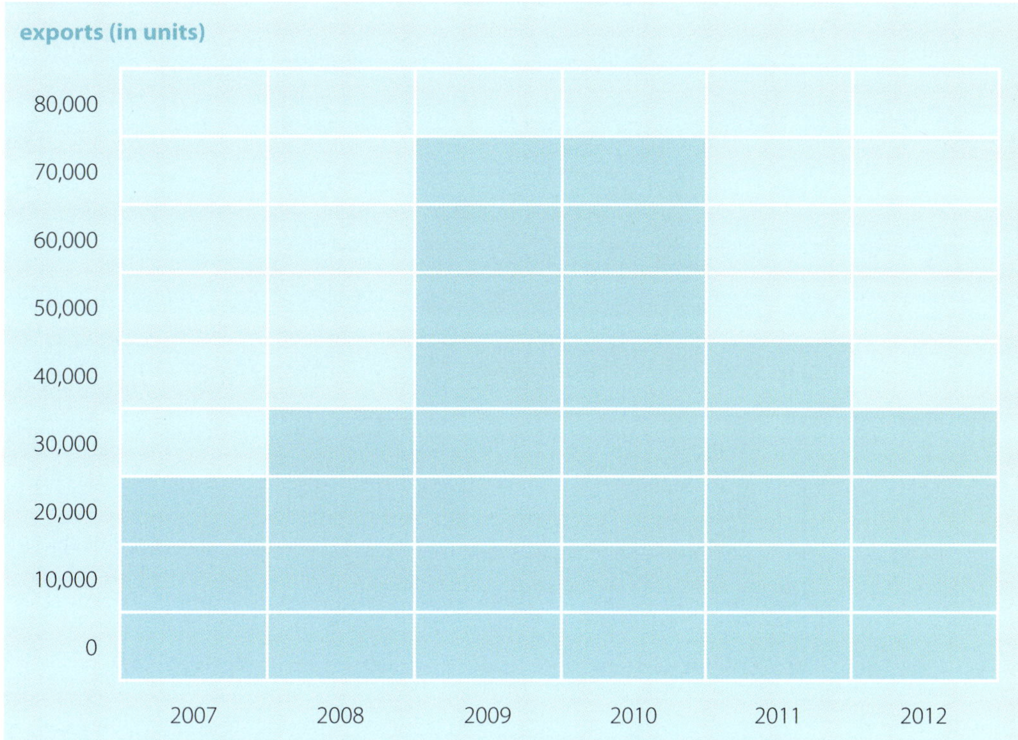

2 Look at the table. It shows ways you can talk about information in a graph. Look at the bar graph in exercise 1 again, and write the correct year in the table. Then take turns reading the sentences with a partner.

Exports	increased	sharply slightly	in 2009 ______
	decreased	sharply slightly	from ______ to ______ in ______
	stayed about the same from ______ to		

3 2.03 Listen to Andrea giving a presentation about the number of customer complaints her department received last year. Draw in the correct bars on the graph.

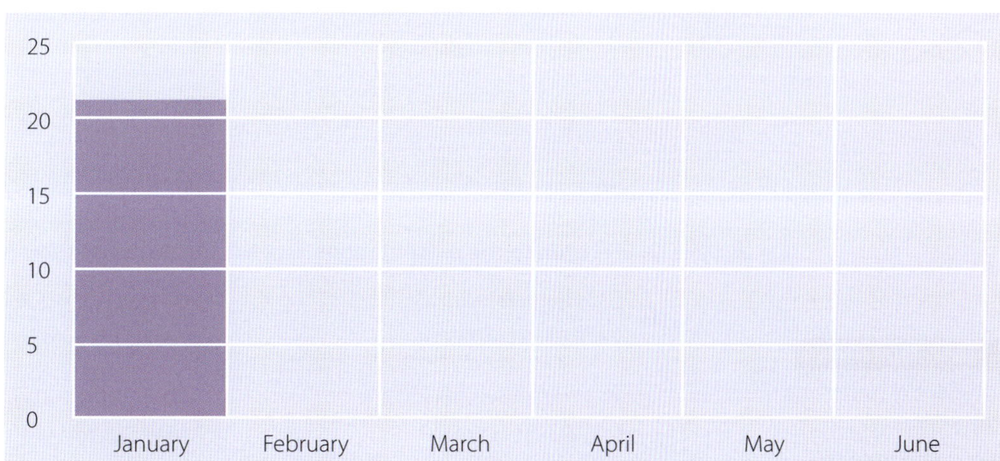

Giving a presentation

1 Look at these sentences that people use when they give presentations. When do you think people say them? Copy the sentences into the correct place in the table.

OK, can everybody see?

Is everybody here?

Is everybody with me so far?

We're finished for today.

Let's get started.

Let's take a five-minute break.

As you can see here, …

That's all for now.

Thanks for listening.
Are there any questions?

At the beginning	In the middle	At the end

2 2.04 Listen to the presentations. Tick (✓) the sentences you hear.

a ☐ Let's get started.
☐ We'll begin at 10:00.

b ☐ As you can see here, …
☐ Can everybody see?

c ☐ Are there any questions so far?
☐ Is everybody with me so far?

d ☐ That's all for today.
☐ I think we're finished.

Talk business

Student A, turn to page 93.
Student B, turn to page 105.

Answering questions

1 2.05 After a presentation, we often ask our audience if there are any questions. But what happens if you don't know the answer? Listen to these ways you can respond. Then practise with a partner.

A: Excuse me, how much will the new computers cost?

B: **I'm sorry, I'm not really sure. I'll check on that and get back to you.**

A: Thanks, I'd appreciate that.

A: When is the next training session?

B: **I'm sorry, I don't know. I'll check with** Pam **and let you know.**

A: OK, thanks.

A: Is this information available in a document?

B: **Actually, I'm not sure. Let me check on that for you.**

A: Oh, that's OK, it's not important.

2 Work with a partner. Take turns asking the questions and responding. Use the conversations in exercise 1 as models.

a What's the population of Russia?

b Who is the Prime Minister of Australia?

c How much does an average apartment in Paris cost?

d When was the internet invented?

e How many people speak Mandarin?

f What are the official languages of Sri Lanka?

g What is the CEO's salary?

h How many employees are there in Taiwan?

Viewpoints Presentations

1 Read what these people say about giving and attending presentations. Which kinds of presentations have you given or attended?

Mei-ling Chen,
Project Manager, Singapore

We have customers from many different companies, so our presentations are in English. We use a lot of charts and graphs to make sure everyone understands the information. Some of our presentations are pretty long, so we sometimes take a tea break in the middle.

Tasha Green,
Administrative Assistant, US

These days, most people use some kind of presentation software like PowerPoint®. Sometimes the presentations look really good, but I don't like it when people just read their slides to you. That's boring.

Viktor Brodsky,
CEO, Ukraine

I prefer to just talk during my presentations. I don't want to worry about using equipment and graphs and charts. If you depend on equipment and it doesn't work, then what happens to your presentation?

2 Which kinds of presentations do you like? Put a tick (✓) on the bar closest to your opinion. Then talk about your opinions in a group. (If you haven't attended or given any presentations, answer about a school class.)

			no opinion; either is fine ↓			
I like long presentations.	☐	☐	☐	☐	☐	I like short presentations.
It's OK if I don't know the topic in advance.	☐	☐	☐	☐	☐	I want to know the topic in advance.
Eating and drinking is distracting.	☐	☐	☐	☐	☐	I like to drink coffee or tea, or have a snack.
Only the presenter should talk.	☐	☐	☐	☐	☐	Everyone should give their opinions.
The atmosphere should be formal. I don't like a lot of joking around.	☐	☐	☐	☐	☐	I like an informal atmosphere. It's OK if the presenter tells some jokes.
People should ask questions at the end of the presentation.	☐	☐	☐	☐	☐	People should ask questions whenever they think of them.
I like just listening during a presentation – no visual aids.	☐	☐	☐	☐	☐	I prefer some kind of visual aid, like PowerPoint® or a graph or chart.

In business Give a presentation

Scenario: You have been asked to give a presentation to a visiting group of people from a company in Brazil. Prepare and give your presentation.

1 Choose some information about your company that you would like to present.

- Sales figures from one year
- Sales figures from more than one year
- Types of products that your company has
- The budget for one department
- The number of imports or exports over a period of several months or years
- The number of employees who work in each department in your company
- The number or type of customer complaints
- Your own idea ______________________________

2 Draw a pie chart or a graph to present your information. Use this space or design it on a computer.

3 Work in groups or with the whole class. Take turns giving a presentation. Don't forget to start and end your presentation with the language on page 66, and to check understanding during your presentation. After you have listened to your classmates' presentations, ask them questions.

UNIT 11

I'm leaving tomorrow

Aims

- Confirming next steps
- Talking about future plans
- Degrees of certainty
- Viewpoints: Talking about the future
- In business: Describe future plans

Listen and practise   Confirming next steps

1 Describe the photos. What is happening?

2 2.06 Scott and Andrew are meeting. Listen to the conversation. Write T for true or F for false next to each sentence.

a Scott will send the contract by the 5th. ______

b Andrew is leaving this weekend. ______

3 2.06 Listen again and complete the conversation. Then practise with a partner. Take turns being Scott and Andrew.

Scott: OK, let me confirm our next steps. ______ ______ ______ send us a cost estimate by the end of this week. Is that right?

Andrew: That's right, and ______ ______ prepare the contract?

Scott: Yes, we'll send it to you by the 15th. Is that OK?

Andrew: That's great. ______ ______ working on this right away.

Scott: Great! ______ ______ ______ back this weekend?

Andrew: Yes, I'm leaving tomorrow morning.

Scott: What ______ ______ ______ this evening?

Andrew: Nothing special. I'm going to pack my suitcases.

4 Practise the conversation again. Change the information in blue using the ideas below.

a deliver the parts this afternoon / prepare the invoice / by Friday

b arrange a meeting by the 12th / make the agenda / by tomorrow

c meet the customer tomorrow / check the address / today

d finish the report by five o'clock / send the data / by lunchtime

5 2.07 What do you think Scott will say next? Tick (✓) your guesses. Then listen to see if you are correct.

a ☐ Where is your hotel?
b ☐ Have a good flight!
c ☐ How many suitcases do you have?
d ☐ Would you like to have dinner?

Talking about future plans

1 Look at the table. It shows ways you can talk about future plans.

Form	Example	Meaning
will	I will finish the report tomorrow.	intention, promise
	Don't worry, I'll help you.	just decided
be going to	We're going to meet him today.	already planned
verb + *-ing*	I'm leaving tomorrow.	already planned (usually near future)

2 2.08 Listen to these five conversations. Match the conversation with the picture. Number the pictures in order 1–5.

a ☐
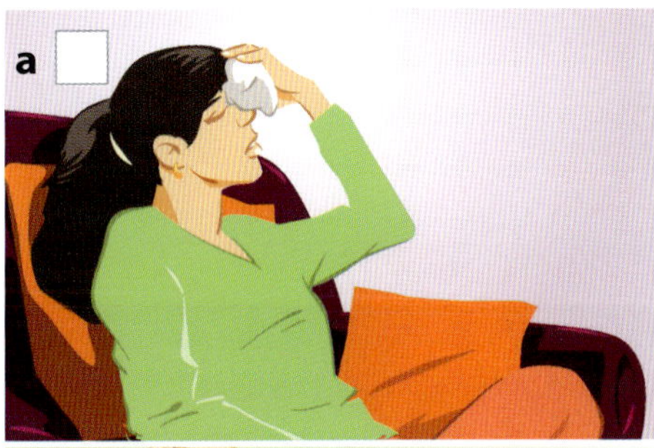

b ☐

c ☐

d ☐
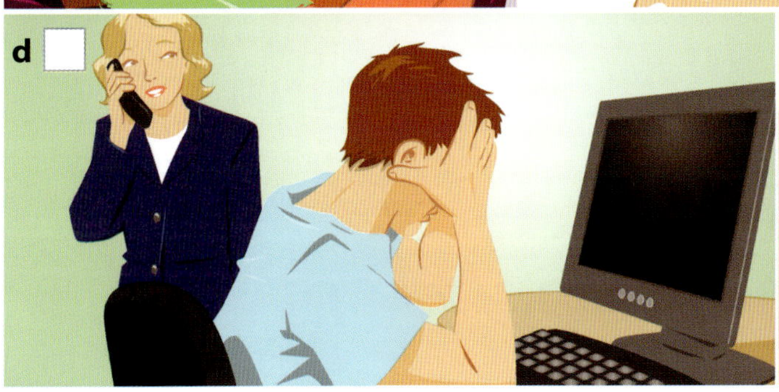

e ☐

3 2.08 Listen again and complete these sentences from the conversations. Check your answers with a partner.

a Don't worry, ___*I'll help*___ you find it. (help)
b 6:30. ______________ a taxi to the airport. (take)
c My friends ______________ at the airport. (meet)
d I'm too tired. ______________ tomorrow. (go shopping)
e Tomorrow ______________ a barbecue. (have)
f On Sunday ______________ my flat. (clean up)
g I'm not sure. Perhaps ______________ a film. (watch)
h Just a minute, ______________ the help desk. (call)

4 Look at the table. It shows ways you can ask about future plans. With a partner, ask about future plans. Then change partners and repeat the exercise.

What are you going to do What are you doing	tomorrow? next week? tonight? next Sunday?

5 Here are some other verbs you can use to talk about future plans. With a different partner, talk about your plans for three, five, and ten years from now.

For example:

Five years from now I hope to work in France.

Three years from now,	I	plan to am planning to	visit London. buy a house. be the Sales Manager.
		hope to am hoping to	

6 2.09 Listen and draw lines to connect the company with their plans. Describe the plans. Then check your answers with a partner.

a	Marco Supermarkets	increase sales in Asia	next year
b	Ruhr Pipe Manufacturing	open four more stores	this year
c	Timson Watches	hire more staff	in the next two years
d	Aztec Coffee	build a new plant	three years from now

Talk business

Student A, turn to page 94.

Student B, turn to page 106.

Degrees of certainty

1 Look at the table. It shows adverbs you can use to show how certain we are about something.

definitely	definitely not	stronger
probably	probably not	↓
perhaps / maybe	perhaps not / maybe not	weaker

2 In groups of three, ask and answer these questions.

For example: A: *Do you think it'll rain tomorrow?*
B: *Maybe. How about you?*
A: *Probably not. What do you think?*
C: *Definitely not.*

1 Do you think it'll rain next weekend?
2 Do you think you'll travel overseas next year?
3 Do you think you'll work for a big company?

3 Look at these sentences; they show the position of the adverb. Practise saying them with a partner.

I'll **definitely** send the invoice today.	I **definitely** won't finish the report today.
We're **probably** going to visit Malaysia next week.	We're **probably** not going to the meeting next week.

Perhaps I'll take a day off tomorrow.
Maybe I'll visit New York next year.
Do you think you'll visit the factory next week? I **probably** will.

4 How sure are you about these statements? Talk about your answers in a group.

a I'll live overseas.

b I'll run a marathon next year.

c In five years I'll be on TV.

d I'll use English in my job.

Viewpoints Talking about the future

1 2.10 Listen to people from three different countries talking about their futures. Write down the degree of certainty next to their plans.

Ji-young Kim, Office Worker, Korea

I'll *definitely* stay with this company.

I'll ________ be sent to the US to study.

________ I will be a manager.

I'll ________ get married sometime.

I ________ want to continue working after I'm married.

Amnuay Chaichan, Assistant Sales Manager, Thailand

I'll ________ travel around Europe.

I ________ want to take my family with me.

Julie Howe, Construction Worker, Canada

________ I'll work in the US for a few years.

I ________ want to come back to Canada.

2 In groups of three, pretend you are one of the people in exercise 1. Tell the others about your future plans.

3 Do you know what you want to do in the future? What are some of your future hopes, plans, and dreams? Make some notes in the table below. Talk about your future plans in a small group.

Time frame	Event / Action

In business Describe future plans

Scenario: You have been asked to give a presentation to investors in your company about your plans for the future.

1 Work with a partner or in groups of three. Choose one of the following industries (or use your own idea).

Car Manufacturing	Cosmetics	Cellphone Manufacturing
Fast-food Restaurants	E-learning: English online	Your own idea:

2 With your partner or group, decide what kind of company it is (for example, how many employees you have, what type of products you sell or make, where your head office is, how many offices you have).

3 Think about how your company will change over the next three, five and ten years. Discuss these questions and make notes.

- Are you going to expand your business?
- Are you going to open overseas offices?
- Are you going to hire more people?
- Are you planning to make different products?

4 Complete the table below with your ideas. You may also like to make some graphs and charts to show your ideas.

Time frame	Event / Action

5 Present your plans to your group or class. Begin like this:

Thanks for coming today. I'm going to talk about our future plans. First …

UNIT 12

Would you like to try some dim sum?

Aims

- Entertaining guests
- Offering and accepting or refusing food
- Giving and receiving compliments
- Thanking and responding to thanks
- Viewpoints: Food and business entertaining
- In business: Planning a social event

Listen and practise Entertaining guests

1 Describe the photo.

2 2.11 Listen to some business people entertaining their guests. Tick (✓) the foods and drinks they mention.

☐ chicken	☐ coffee	☐ salad
☐ vegetables	☐ shrimp	☐ tea

3 2.11 Listen again and complete the conversation. Then practise with a partner. Take turns being Lily and Grace.

Lily: ________ you ________ to try some dim sum?

Grace: Yes, thank you, they ________ delicious. Um, what's ________ them?

Lily: These ones have ________ , and these ones have ________ .

Grace: And, uh, ________ do I eat them?

Lily: Oh, it's ________ . You ________ one ________ with your chopsticks… like this… and dip it into the sauce.

4 Practise the conversation again. Change the information in blue using the ideas below.

a tacos / beef, beans and cheese / hand / just eat it

b samosas / potatoes, meat / fork / put it on your plate

c sushi / cucumber, fish / chopsticks / dip it in soy sauce

5 2.12 What do you think Lily will do next? Tick (✓) your guesses. Then listen to see if you are correct.

a ☐ She will offer Grace something to drink.
b ☐ She will ask Grace if she likes the dim sum.
c ☐ She will tell Grace how to make dim sum.
d ☐ She will ask Grace to pass her some food.

Offering and accepting or refusing food

1 Look at the tables. They show ways you can offer food, and accept or refuse food. Practise with a partner. Take turns reading the questions and answers.

Questions:	
Would you like to try*	a taco?
Would you like	a cup of coffee? some crisps? some (more) cake?

*(**Note:** *Use* ***to try*** *if your guest has not had the food before.)*

Answers:		
Yes, please.	It looks They smell That sounds	delicious. wonderful. good.
No, thank you.	I just had one / some. I can't eat any more!	
	I'm	a vegetarian. allergic. on a diet.

2 2.13 Listen to these conversations. Tick (✓) the question that you hear. Then write the response.

a ☐ Would you like some …?
☐ Would you like to try some …?

____

b ☐ Would you like some more …?
☐ Would you like to try some …?

____

c ☐ Would you like a …?
☐ Would you like some …?

____

d ☐ Would you like some …?
☐ Would you like some more …?

____

3 Practise with a partner. Take turns offering these foods and drinks and accepting or refusing them. Use the information below and your own ideas.

a some pizza

c some chicken curry

b a brownie

d an apple

Giving and receiving compliments

1 2.14 Listen to the conversations.

Conversation 1

Guest: This fish is delicious!

Host: No, it isn't. It's too salty and dry.

Guest: Oh. Well, it tastes good to me …

Conversation 2

Guest: This curry is delicious!

Host: Oh, thank you. My daughter made it with me. I hope it's not too spicy.

Guest: No, not at all. What's in it?

Host: Well, chicken, fresh vegetables, and my own spices. Would you like the recipe?

Guest: Yes, thank you. That's very kind of you.

2 Discuss these questions with a partner.

a In which conversation does the guest feel uncomfortable? Why? Practise the successful conversation.

b In English, it is common to give compliments. If you receive a compliment, it is polite to accept it (*Thank you*) and then say one or two more sentences about the item that is being complimented (*My daughter made it with me. I hope it's not too spicy.*). What is the custom in your culture?

(**Note:** Do not give compliments on a person's personal appearance. You might hurt someone's feelings, or give the wrong impression. Women can compliment other women on their clothing or accessories, but men should not give these kinds of compliments to women.)

Talk business

Student A, turn to page 95.

Student B, turn to page 107.

3 Practise with a partner. Take turns giving and accepting compliments. Use the information below and then your own ideas. Use a polite tone of voice!

a garden is lovely / wife planted the roses

c coffee is delicious / from Guatemala

b town is beautiful / many old buildings

d son is very smart / only two years old

Thanking and responding to thanks

1 Look at the table. Then practise with a partner. Take turns thanking and responding.

Thank you for	lunch the flowers.	You're welcome. I'm glad you liked it / them. Oh, don't mention it. Oh, not at all.
	inviting me. sending me the report.	

2 Work in a group. Take turns thanking every group member for something. Respond to your classmates' thanks in a different way each time.

Thank you for being my partner.

You're welcome.

Thank you for making me laugh.

Oh, don't mention it.

Viewpoints Food and business entertaining

1 Read what these people from around the world say about food. Which culture is most similar to yours?

Rajiv Das,
Business man, India

Business lunches are more common than business dinners. If you are served traditional Indian food, remember to eat only with the right hand – even if you are left-handed! In addition, do not use your hands to take food from a communal dish. Muslims do not eat pork, and Hindus do not eat beef, so vegetarian dishes are common.

Dmitri Petrov,
Product Planner, Russia

Russians appreciate a good supply of different snacks and drinks at business meetings. Both the food and the serving dishes (plates, cups, and so on) should be of good quality. If you are invited to a Russian's home, you will be offered a lot of food! It is polite to bring a gift if you are the guest.

Lucia Dominguez,
CEO, Argentina

Business entertaining is very common. We usually invite guests to dinner at a restaurant, not a private home. We don't talk about business over dinner, though – it's a time to get to know one another on a social level. Meat, especially local beef, is a popular dish. Dinners start at around 10:00pm.

2 What kind of foods do you like to eat on these occasions? Make a quick list.

for breakfast	while watching TV	for dessert	when I'm unhappy	at a birthday party	at a sporting event

3 Compare your answers in a group. How would you explain any foods that an international visitor would not know? Tell the group. Do you all enjoy the same kinds of food?

In business Planning a social event

Scenario: You have been asked by your boss to plan a social event for your company.

1 Discuss the following questions in a group.

- What is the reason for the party?
- Who will you invite?
- What kind of entertainment will you have?
- What kind of food will you serve?

snacks	food	drinks

Report back your ideas to the group or class.

2 Role-play your party in a group or with the whole class. Use this conversation map.

Host:	Guest:
Offer some food or drink. →	Accept or Refuse (say why).
← If the guest refuses, offer something else until the guest accepts. →	Compliment the food or drink.
← Accept the compliment and give more information. →	Thank the host.
← Accept the thanks. →	Say goodbye.
← Say goodbye.	

Review: Units 9–12

1 Where's it from?

Match the food to the country. Then use the conversation map to offer and accept.

1 
England

2 
Japan

3 
Italy

4 
the US

5 
China

a 
sushi

b 
hamburger

c 
dim sum

d 
roast beef

e 
pasta

Host:		Guest:
Offer some food.	→	Accept. Ask where it's from.
Respond.	←	
	→	Compliment the food.
Accept the compliment.	←	

2 Finish the graph!

Complete the graph and add a title. Describe the graph to a partner.

As you can see here…

Let's get started.

This graph shows…

3 What's the next step?

2.15 Listen and complete the steps in the process. Then describe the process to a partner.

a c ___ ___ ___ ___ ___ ___ ___ o ___ ___ ___ ___

b m ___ ___ ___ ___ ___ ___ t ___ ___ ___ ___ g

c t ___ ___ ___ ___ n ___

d s ___ ___ ___ ___ ___ ___ g

4 Great job!

Match the compliment with the response. Then practise with a partner.

a I enjoyed your presentation!	Thank you. We moved here last month.
b I like your bag!	Thank you! They're chocolate chip. My daughter made them.
c These are nice offices!	Thank you. It was a present from my mother.
d These are delicious!	Thank you! It took me a long time to make the slides.

5 Q&A

With a partner ask and answer questions about the graph.
Then student A gives an answer, and student B makes the question.

For example:
Q *How many people joined FM Fashion last year?*
A *102.*

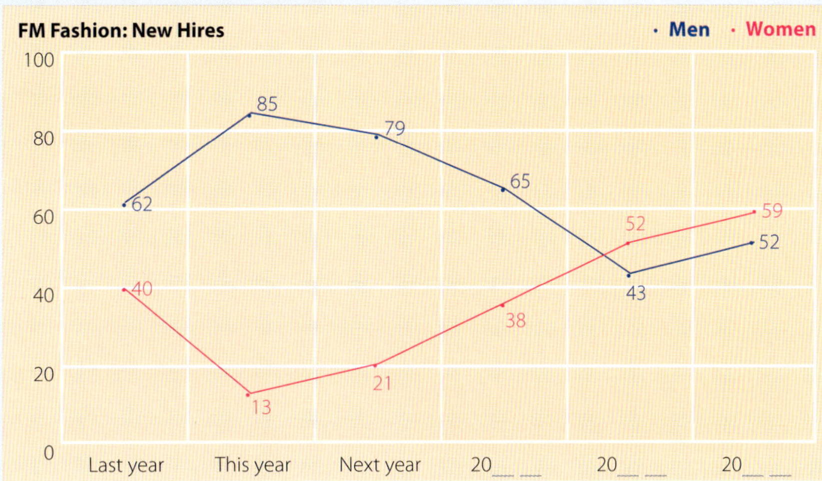

For example:
A *38.*
Q *How many women will probably join FM Fashion in 20_ _?*

6 Don't mention it.

2.16 Jill wants to thank you. Listen and respond when you hear the beep.

7 I'll definitely climb Mt. Everest!

What are your plans for next year? Complete the sentences. Compare your answers with a partner.

Next year	I'll definitely	
	I'll probably	
	perhaps I'll	
	maybe I'll	

Talk business

Student A: use this page Student B: use page 96

Useful language

What	do	you	do?
Who	are do	you	with work for?
What	is	your	address? postcode? phone number? email address?

1 Ask questions to complete student B's business card below. Write B's responses.

Chris Chandler
production ________

________ **Media Services**

We produce top-quality videos

66 ________ Street
Dublin 7
(01) 484 ________
________@________

2 Answer student B's questions about your business card.

PACIFIC FINANCE

Mary Chan
Marketing Manager

Personal Banking Services

105 Thomson Road ... Tel: 6355 5749
33-05 United Square ... Fax: 6355 6763
Singapore 309875
email: chan_c@pacfinance.com

3 Compare your books. Did you get the correct information?

Talk business

Student A: use this page Student B: use page 97

Useful language	
Do you	write emails? take part in one-on-one meetings? take part in teleconferences?
How often do you	give presentations? make telephone calls? go on overseas business trips?

1 Ask student B questions to complete the survey about B's on-the-job use of English. Write B's responses.

Asia Research Centre – Survey of on-the-job use of English

Activity	Yes / No	How often?
read emails		
write emails		
take part in one-on-one meetings		
take part in group meetings		
use the telephone		
take part in teleconferences		
give presentations		
go on overseas business trips		
other: *welcome foreign visitors*		

2 Answer student B's questions. Use this information.

Asia Research Centre – Survey of on-the-job use of English

Activity	Yes / No	How often?
read emails	Yes	every day
write emails	Yes	every day
take part in one-on-one meetings	Yes	once a month
take part in group meetings	Yes	two or three times a month
use the telephone	Yes	every day
take part in teleconferences	No	–
give presentations	No	–
go on overseas business trips	No	–
other: *give factory tours*	Yes	every month

3 Compare your books. Did you get the correct information?

Talk business

Student A: use this page Student B: use page 98

Useful language				
What		does	your company	do?
Where		is	your head office?	
When		was	the company	established?
How many	offices employees	do	you	have?

1 Ask student B questions to get information about Rock On! Records. Complete the table.

Rock On! Records	
Head office:	
Established:	
Employees:	
Offices:	
Factories:	
Business:	

2 Answer student B's questions about Fujimoto Heavy Industries.

Fujimoto Heavy Industries	
Head office:	Kawasaki, Japan
Established:	1946
Employees:	32,097
Offices:	Kawasaki, Tokyo, Osaka
Factories:	Kawasaki, Sasebo
Business:	builds ships, makes airplanes

3 Compare your books. Did you get the correct information?

Talk business

Student A: use this page Student B: use page 99

Useful language

You should … Why don't you … ? I recommend … How about … ?	That's a good idea, thanks. Well, maybe.

1 Tell student B your problems. Listen to B's suggestions.

If you like the suggestion, say, 'That's a good idea, thanks.'

If you don't like the suggestion, say, 'Well, maybe.'

a I feel very sleepy now.
b I don't understand this word.
c I want to buy a cheap plane ticket.
d I usually miss my morning bus.
e I need some more money.

2 Listen to student B's problems. Make suggestions using the information below.

ride your bicycle to work give it to me read the manual	go shopping with me try to relax more ask one of your classmates

Talk business

Student A: use this page Student B: use page 100

Useful language

How do you spell (that)?
Can you speak more slowly?
Can you speak more loudly?
Can you repeat that?
Can you say that again?

1 You are the caller.

You are Chris Patterson at J&B Productions.
Your phone number is 077 – 9888 – 6533.

Call student B and ask for Jennifer Cho. If she is not there, leave a message. Ask her to call you back tomorrow morning.

Begin the call by saying: *'Ring, ring.'*

2 You are the receiver.

You will receive a phone call from student B. You are the receptionist for NBI. Ms Thompson is in a meeting.

Take a message using the form below. Remember to thank the caller and end the phone call!

Telephone Message

To: Margaret Thompson

From:

Tel:

☐ please call back ☐ other
☐ will call you back

Message:

Taken by: TIme:

3 Compare your books. Did you get the correct information?

Talk business

Student A: use this page **Student B: use page 101**

Practise the conversation below. Then have similar conversations using the information in the charts.

A: *Do you know which (camera) is (cheaper)?*

B: *Well, (the XLR) is ($300). How about the (Ricon 900)?*

A: *That one is ($500).*

B: *OK, then (the XLR) is (cheaper). You should get that one.*

1 Ask shopper B about the smartphone, the English book, and the video game.

Begin like this: *Do you know which smartphone is lighter?*

1 smartphone – light

the Blueberry: ___ grams

the Strawberry: 5 grams

2 English book – short

Great Grammar: ___ pages

Grammar Fun: 128 pages

3 video game – good

Space Battle: ___ stars

Educational Journey: 2 stars

2 Talk with shopper B about the suit, the CD, and the ladder. (B starts.)

4 suit – expensive

the Yugo Moss: $900

the Nolo: $___

5 CD – new

Radio Hits: 20 years old

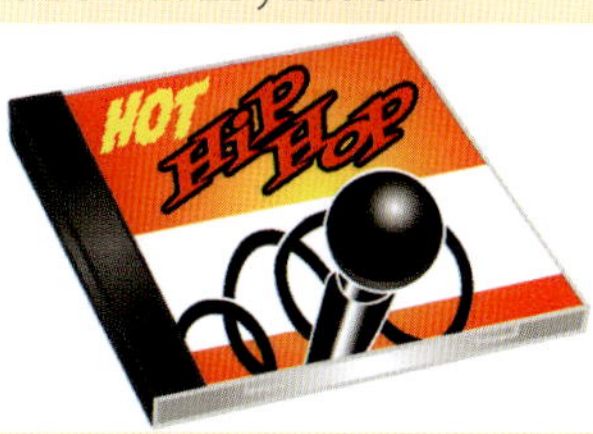

Hot Hip Hop: ___ years old

6 ladder – tall

the grey one: 3 metres long

the black one: ___ metres long

3 Compare your books. Did you get the correct information?

Talk business

Student A: use this page Student B: use page 102

Let me confirm. Let me repeat that.	That's … . You said … . The … is … .	Is that right?

1 Caller 

You are Mary Chan.

You are calling the Pacific Restaurant. You want to make a lunch reservation.

Restaurant: (Student B)

You: Hello, I'd like to make a reservation, please.

This is your reservation information:

12:45 Pacific Restaurant 14th Dec
5 adults, 3 children
Mobile phone: 075 3333 8570

2 Receiver 

You are Anna Martinez at BL Chemicals

You will receive a phone call from Mikel Deuter at Ruhr Pipe. Write down his order in the form. (Remember to check the information!)

You: Hello, BL Chemicals. How can I help you?

Mikel Deuter: (Student B)

You: Certainly. Can you give me the part numbers and quantity, Mr Deuter?

Mikel Deuter: …………

You: Thank you for your order, Mr Deuter. I will send you an email today to confirm this information.

BL Chemicals: Order Form

Part Number	Quantity

3 Compare your books. Did you get the correct information?

Talk business

Student A: use this page Student B: use page 103

Useful language

Where is the ______________ ?
It's …

across from   behind   between   in front of
in the corner   next to / on the left
next to / on the right   under

1 Look at the map of the shopping centre below. Ask student B where these shops are, and write them onto the map: *ice cream shop, video game arcade, furniture shop, cosmetics shop.*

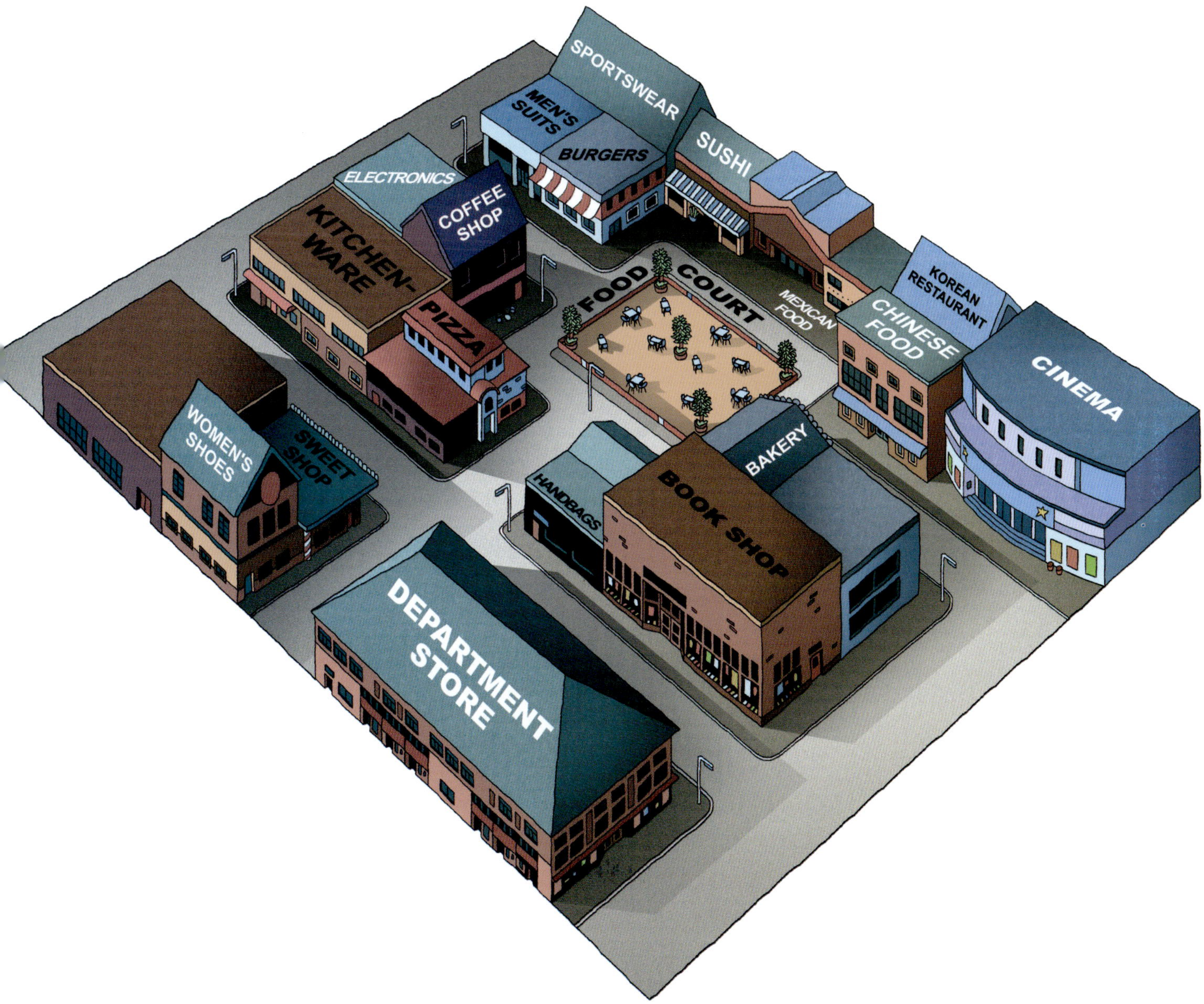

2 Answer student B's questions.

3 Compare your books. Did you get the right information?

Talk business

Student A: use this page Student B: use page 104

1 Describe the first part of the process to student B. Check that he / she understands.

Begin like this:
The first step is to research the company. For example, what are their products? …

Useful language

Is that clear (so far)?
Are you with me (so far)?
OK?

Preparing for a job interview.

1 Research the company	What are their products? Who are their main customers?
2 Plan your route	Where is the office? How long does it take to get there?
3 Practise	Prepare answers: What are your strengths / weaknesses / future dreams?
4 Dress right	Look professional. Get a haircut.

2 Listen to student B's description and complete the second part of the process. Check and confirm that you understand.

Useful language

Yes, that's clear. I understand. OK. I'm with you.	Let me repeat that … Let me confirm …

5 ________ early	________ ________ minutes early. ________ off your mobile phone.
6 ________ ________ shy!	Talk about your experiences. ________ ________ who you are!
7 ________ ________	Ask about the company and ________ ________ . Ask about ________ plans.
8 Follow-up	________ ________: Send a thank-you note or ________ .

3 Compare your books. Did you get the correct information?

Talk business

Student A: use this page Student B: use page 105

Here is information about visitors to the Grand Canyon in Arizona, US.

1 a Complete the pie chart. Ask student B for information like this:

What percentage of visitors to the Grand Canyon were (...)?

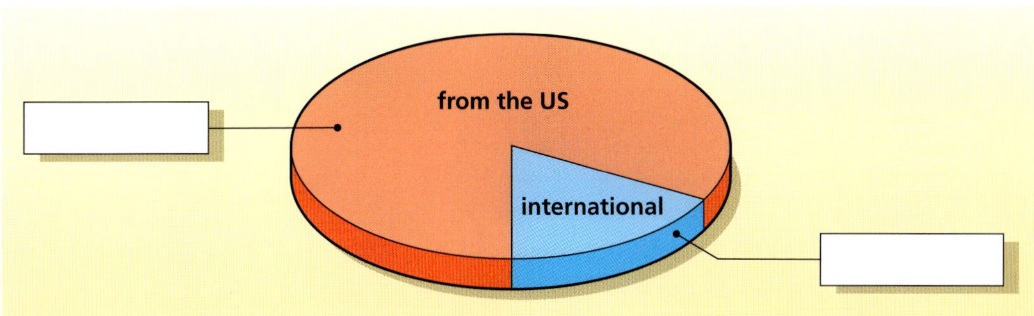

b Complete the bar graph by drawing in the correct bars for each country. Ask student B for information like this:

How many people came from (...)?

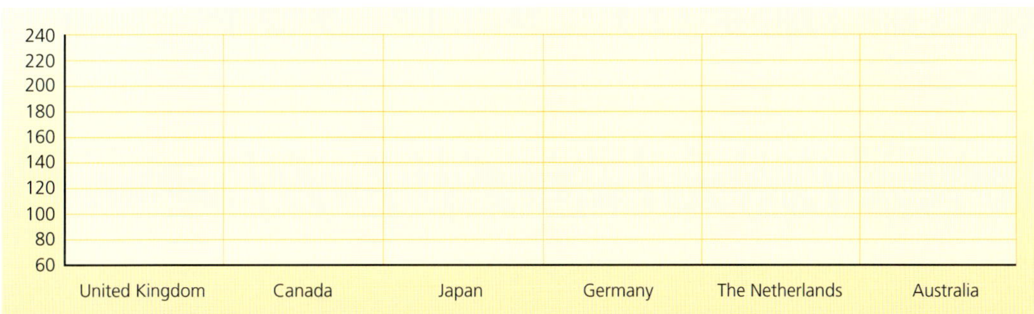

2 Answer student B's questions with this information:

a Most visitors to the Grand Canyon National Park, 58.6 percent, were first-time visitors. 41.4 percent were repeat visitors, or visitors who had been to the park before.

b

State	Number of visitors
California	739
Arizona	535
Texas	288
Florida	204
New York	195
Ohio	190

3 Compare your books. Did you get the correct information?

Talk business

Student A: use this page Student B: use page 106

Useful language

From January to February we In March we	will … are going to … plan to … hope to …

1 Describe the development schedule to student B. Check that he / she understands.

Project XPII – Development Schedule

Time Frame	Action / Event
March – July	Design the parts
July – September	Build a prototype
August – October	Test the prototype
October – November	Contact suppliers
December	Decide on a supplier
January	Plan the production schedule
February	Start production

2 Listen to student B's description and complete the chart. Remember to confirm that you understand.

	Month														
	A	M	J	J	A	S	O	N	D	J	F	M	A	M	J
Advertise (website)															
Colleges / Universities															
Career Fairs															
Group Interviews															
One-on-one Interviews															
Job Offers															
New Employee Orientation															
New Employee Training															

3 Compare your books. Did you get the correct information?

Talk business

Student A: use this page Student B: use page 107

Useful language	
A: Would you like a / some (____)?	B: Sure. Where is it / are they from?
A: It's / They're from (____).	B: What's in it / them?
A: (____).	B: Thank you. It looks / They look delicious.

1 Offer student B these dishes. Answer B's questions.

a summer rolls

summer rolls, Vietnam
rice noodles, shrimp, vegetables

b gravlax

gravlax, Norway
salmon (fish), salt and sugar, mustard

c harira

harira, Morocco
lamb, tomatoes, beans, spices

2 Student B will offer you these dishes. Ask where they are from and what is in them. Then accept the offer.

d shepherd's pie

e pavlova

f pakoras

Talk business

Student B: use this page Student A: use page 84

Useful language			
What	do	you	do?
Who	are do	you	with work for?
What	is	your	address? postcode? phone number? email address?

1 Answer student A's questions about your business card.

Chris Chandler
production assistant

Northwest Media Services

We produce top-quality videos

66 Eccles Street
Dublin 7
(01) 4840703
c_chand@nwmedia.net

2 Ask questions to complete student A's business card below. Write A's responses.

PACIFIC FINANCE

Mary Chan

____

Personal Banking __________________

105 Thomson Road ... Tel: 6355 5749
__________ United Square ... Fax: 6355 ______
Singapore __________
email: _________@_________

3 Compare your books. Did you get the correct information?

Talk business

Student B: use this page Student A: use page 85

Useful language	
Do you	write emails? take part in one-on-one meetings? take part in teleconferences?
How often do you	give presentations? make telephone calls? go on overseas business trips?

1 Answer student A's questions. Use this information.

Asia Research Centre – Survey of on-the-job use of English

Activity	Yes / No	How often?
read emails	Yes	every day
write emails	Yes	once a week
take part in one-on-one meetings	No	–
take part in group meetings	Yes	once a month
use the telephone	No	–
take part in teleconferences	No	–
give presentations	Yes	every month
go on overseas business trips	Yes	twice a year
other: *welcome foreign visitors*	Yes	three or four times a year

2 Ask student A questions to complete the survey about A's on-the-job use of English. Write A's responses.

Asia Research Centre – Survey of on-the-job use of English

Activity	Yes / No	How often?
read emails		
write emails		
take part in one-on-one meetings		
take part in group meetings		
use the telephone		
take part in teleconferences		
give presentations		
go on overseas business trips		
other: *give factory tours*		

3 Compare your books. Did you get the correct information?

Talk business

Student B: use this page Student A: use page 86

Useful language				
What		does	your company	do?
Where		is	your head office?	
When		was	the company	established?
How many	offices employees	do	you	have?

1 Answer student A's questions about Rock On! Records.

Rock On! Records	
Head office:	London, U.K.
Established:	1998
Employees:	214
Offices:	London, New York
Factories:	Tokyo, Zurich
Business:	produces music

2 Ask student A questions to get information about Fujimoto Heavy Industries. Complete the table.

Fujimoto Heavy Industries	
Head office:	
Established:	
Employees:	
Offices:	
Factories:	
Business:	

3 Compare your books. Did you get the correct information?

Talk business

Student B: use this page **Student A: use page 87**

Useful language

You should …	
Why don't you … ?	That's a good idea, thanks.
I recommend …	Well, maybe.
How about … ?	

1 Listen to student A's problems. Make suggestions using the information below.

shop online	get up earlier
buy a new one	check a dictionary
drink some coffee	get a part-time job

2 Tell student A your problems. Listen to A's suggestions.

If you like the suggestion, say, 'That's a good idea, thanks.'

If you don't like the suggestion, say, 'Well, maybe.'

a I need to buy my friend a gift.

b I can't use my digital camera.

c I don't remember my teacher's name.

d I don't like this shirt.

e I need more exercise.

Talk business

Student B: use this page Student A: use page 88

Useful language

How do you spell (that)? Can you speak more slowly? Can you speak more loudly?	Can you repeat that? Can you say that again?

1 You are the receiver.

You will receive a phone call from student A. You are the receptionist for CNS Marketing. Ms Cho is not at her desk now.

Take a message using the form below. Remember to thank the caller and end the phone call!

Telephone Message

To: Jennifer Cho

From:

Tel:

☐ please call back ☐ other

☐ will call you back

Message:

Taken by: TIme:

2 You are the caller.

You are Lisa Gomez at Aztec Coffee.
Your phone number is: 55 – 5286 – 1397.

Call student A and ask for Margaret Thompson. If she is not there, leave a message. Ask her to call you back this afternoon before 5:30.

Begin the call by saying: *'Ring, ring'.*

3 Compare your books. Did you get the correct information?

Talk business

Student B: use this page Student A: use page 89

Practise the conversation below. Then have similar conversations using the information in the charts.

A: *Do you know which (camera) is (cheaper)?*

B: *Well, (the XLR) is ($300). How about the (Ricon 900)?*

A: *That one is ($500).*

B: *OK, then (the XLR) is (cheaper). You should get that one.*

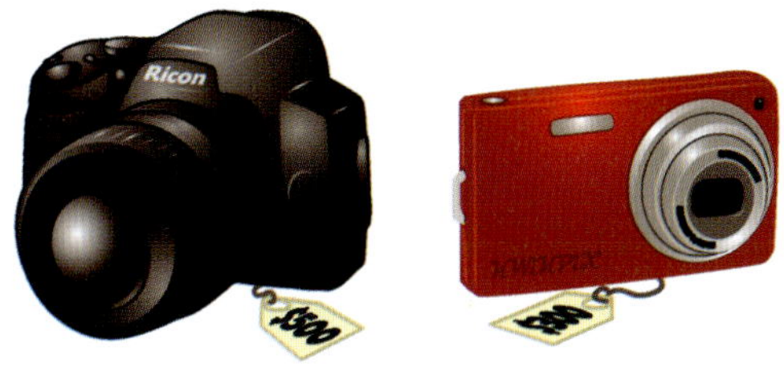

1 Talk with shopper A about the smartphone, the English book, and the video game. (A starts.)

1 smartphone – light

the Blueberry: 3 grams

the Strawberry: ___ grams

2 English book – short

Great Grammar: 380 pages

Grammar Fun: ___ pages

3 video game – good

Space Battle: 5 stars

Educational Journey: ___ stars

2 Ask shopper A about the suit, the CD, and the ladder.

Begin like this: *Do you know which suit is more expensive?*

4 suit – expensive

the Yugo Moss: $___

the Nolo: $2,500

5 CD – new

Radio Hits: ___ years old

Hot Hip Hop: 2 years old

6 ladder – tall

the grey one: ___ metres long

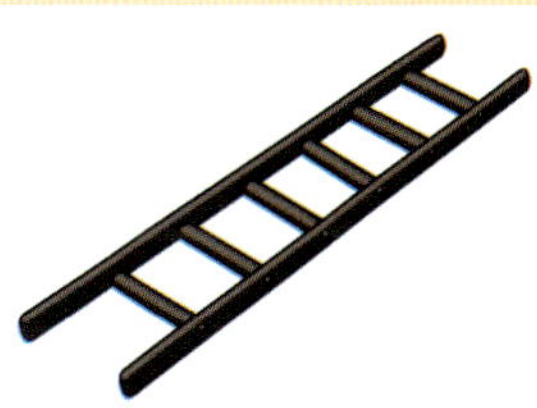

the black one: 2 metres long

3 Compare your books. Did you get the correct information?

Talk business

Student B: use this page Student A: use page 90

Let me confirm. Let me repeat that.	That's .... . You said .... . The ... is	Is that right?

1 Receiver 

You are Jenny Sanderson at Pacific Restaurant.

You will receive a phone call. Write down the reservation information in the form. (Remember to check the information!)

Pacific Restaurant **RESERVATION ORDER**

GUEST NAME: ______ DATE: ______ TIME: ______

NO. OF PEOPLE: ______ ADULTS: ______ CHILDREN: ______

TEL: ______

You: Good morning, Pacific Restaurant. How can I help you?

Mary: (Student A)

You: Certainly. Can I have your name, please?

Mary: ....

You: Thank you for your call. We look forward to serving you.

2 Caller 

You are Mikel Deuter at Ruhr Pipe.

You are calling Anna Martinez at BL Chemicals. You want to order some parts.

Anna: (Student A)

You: Hello, this is Mikel Deuter at Ruhr Pipe. I'd like to order some parts.

Anna: ...

You: Yes, the first one is ...

This is your order:

Need to order from BL Chemicals:

Part No.	Quantity
DD 3245	877
DK 5666Y	2000
YT4176A	619
YT4177D	1500

3 Compare your books. Did you get the correct information?

Talk business

Student B: use this page Student A: use page 91

Useful language	
Where is the ________ ?	across from behind between in front of
It's …	in the corner next to / on the left
	next to / on the right under

1 Look at the map of the shopping centre below. Answer student A's questions.

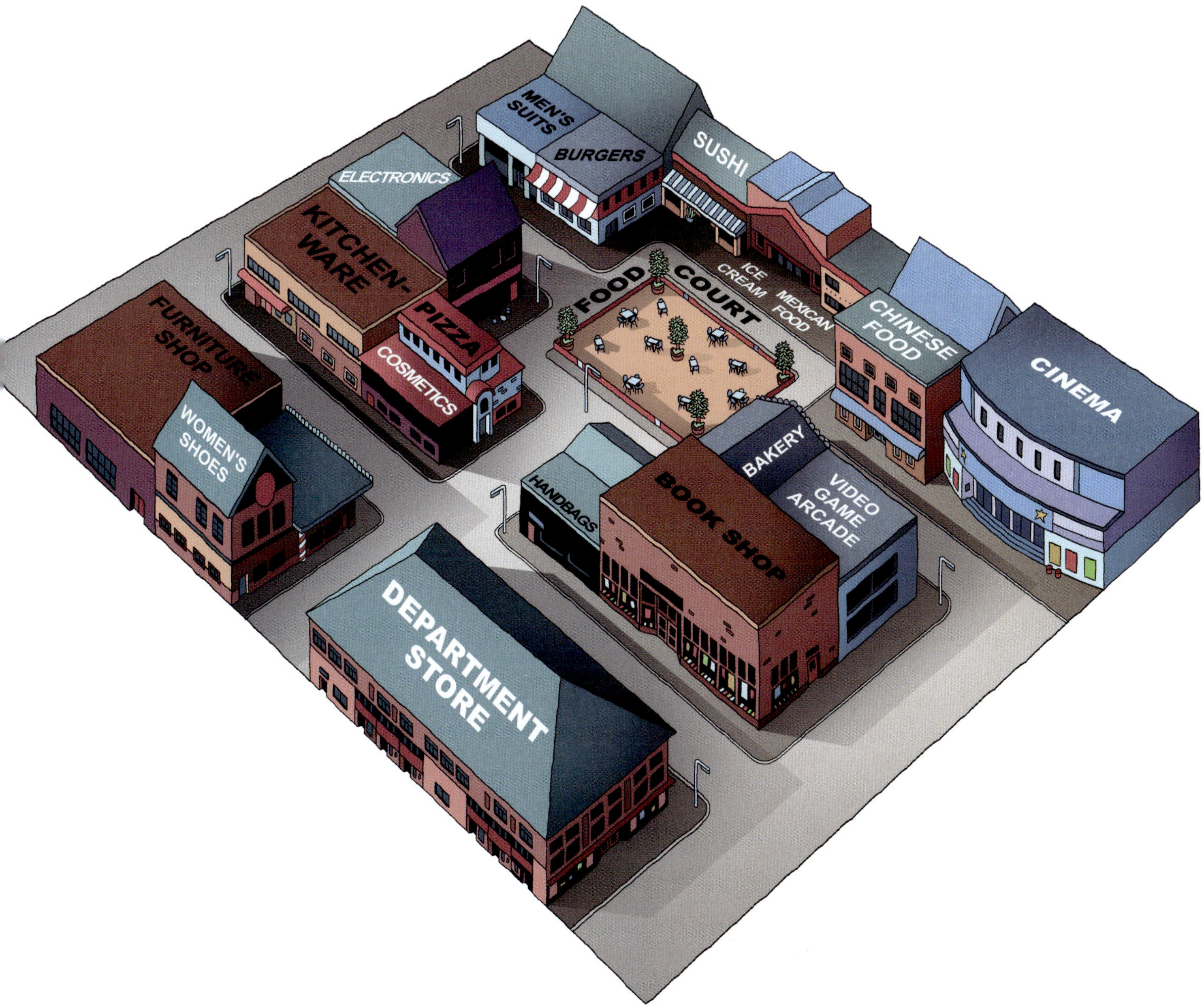

2 Ask student A where these shops are, and write them onto the map: *sweet shop*, *sportswear shop*, *Korean restaurant*, *coffee shop*.

3 Compare your books. Did you get the right information?

Talk business

Student B: use this page **Student A: use page 92**

1 Listen to student A's description and complete the first part of the process. Check and confirm that you understand.

Useful language

Yes, that's clear. I understand. OK. I'm with you.	Let me repeat that … Let me confirm …

Preparing for a job interview.

1 ________ the company	What are ________ ________? Who are their ________ customers?
2 Plan ________ ________	Where is the office? ________ ________ does it take to get there?
3 ________	Prepare answers: What are your ________ / weaknesses / future ________?
4 ________ right	________ ________. Get a haircut.

2 Describe the second part of the process to student A. Check that he / she understands.

Begin like this:
The next step is to arrive early. This means you should be 20 minutes early.

Useful language

Is that clear (so far)?
Are you with me (so far)?
OK?

5 Arrive early	Be 20 minutes early. Turn off your mobile phone.
6 Don't be shy!	Talk about your experiences. Show them who you are!
7 Ask questions.	Ask about the company and the job. Ask about future plans.
8 Follow-up	Next day: Send a thank-you note or email.

3 Compare your books. Did you get the correct information?

Talk business

Student B: use this page Student A: use page 93

Here is information about visitors to the Grand Canyon in Arizona, US.

1 Answer student A's questions with this information:

a Most visitors to Grand Canyon National Park, 83 percent, were from the United States. 17 percent of visitors were international.

b

Country	Number of visitors
United Kingdom	227
Canada	209
Japan	129
Germany	117
The Netherlands	71
Australia	65

2 a Complete the pie chart. Ask student A for information like this:

What percentage of people were (...)?

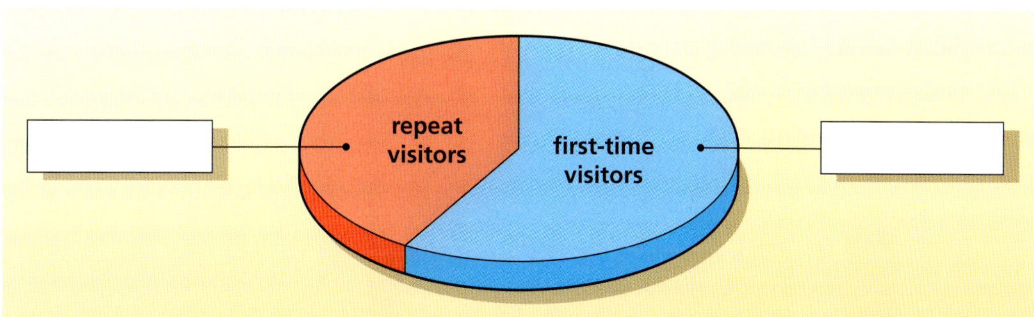

b Complete the bar graph by drawing in the correct bars for each state. Ask student A for information like this:

How many people came from (...)?

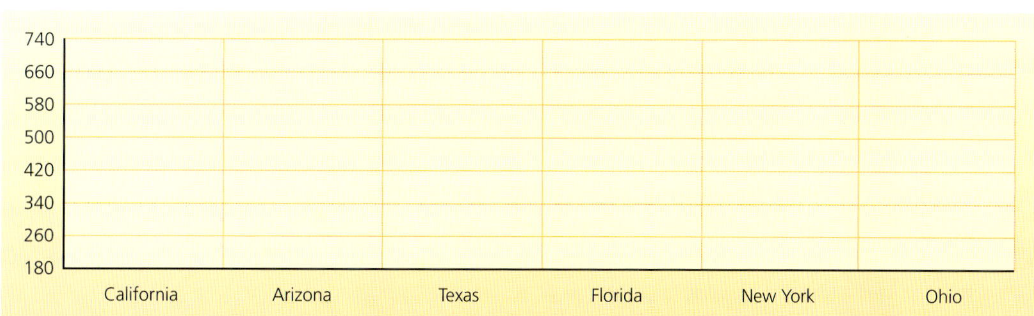

3 Compare your books. Did you get the correct information?

Talk business

Student B: use this page Student A: use page 94

Useful language

From January to February we In March we	will … are going to … plan to … hope to …

1 Listen to student A's description and complete the chart. Remember to confirm that you understand.

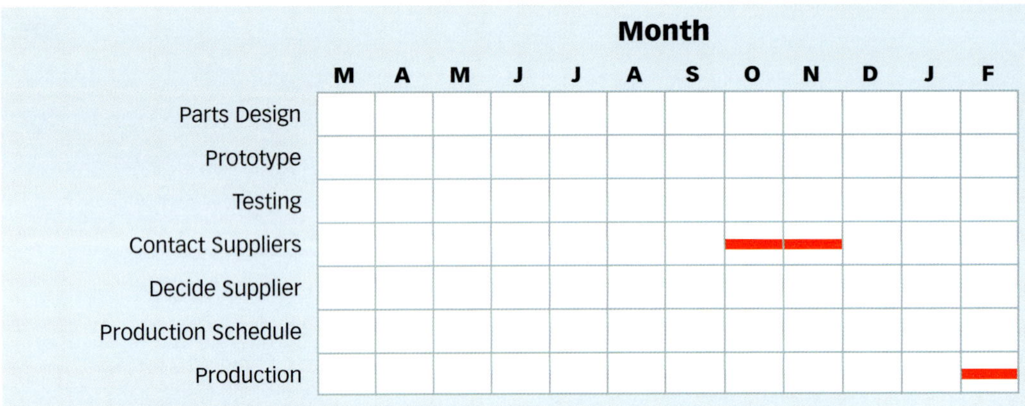

2 Describe the recruiting timeline to student A. Check that he / she understands.

New Employee Recruitment – Timeline

Time Frame	Action / Event
April	Post job openings on the website
May – June	Visit colleges & universities
July	Attend career fairs
July – August	Interview candidates (group)
August – September	Interview candidates (one-on-one)
October – November	Make job offers
April	Give orientation to new employees
April – June	New employee training

3 Compare your books. Did you get the correct information?

Talk business

Student B: use this page Student A: use page 95

Useful language	
A: Would you like a / some (____)?	B: Sure. Where is it / are they from?
A: It's / They're from (____).	B: What's in it / them?
A: (____).	B: Thank you. It looks / They look delicious.

1 Student A will offer you these dishes. Ask where they are from and what is in them. Then accept the offer.

a summer rolls

b gravlax

c harira

2 Offer student A these dishes. Answer A's questions.

d shepherd's pie

shepherd's pie, England
beef or lamb, vegetables covered with mashed potatoes

e pavlova

pavlova, Australia
eggs, vanilla, and a lot of sugar!

f pakoras

pakoras, Pakistan
potatoes, onions, flour fried in oil

UNIT 1

BEC Preliminary practice

Reading Part 1

- Look at questions 1–5.
- In each question, which sentence is correct?
- For each question, mark one letter (A, B or C).

Example

This is part of

(A) an email to the staff of Lambert's.
(B) a newspaper article about business cards.
(C) an advertisement for a company.

The correct answer is C.

*Come to **LAMBERT'S** for your business cards – we have over **4,000** designs*

Telephone message

Pablo - Karen Yates from Dorset Technologies will be here at 2 pm instead of 2.30. She hopes that's OK.

1 Karen Yates will arrive

(A) early. (B) on time. (C) late.

Jerry Stephens

Marketing Manager

CLF Software Ltd • Goldacres House
Hampton Street • Peterborough
PE42 7KM

2 Jerry

(A) … writes computer programmes.
(B) … designs houses.
(C) … sells software.

To: Claudia
From: Roger
Subject: Meeting

Room B17 will be in use, and my office is too small. Can we meet in your office?

3 Roger wants the meeting to be in

(A) Claudia's office.
(B) room B17.
(C) his office.

To: All staff
From: Julie, Human Resources
Subject: Training

New training course in web design.

Contact me to find out more.

4 The email tells staff they can ask Julie for information about

(A) Human Resources.
(B) websites.
(C) a training course.

To: Shilpa
From: Joe
Subject: New customer

Shilpa, we need to talk about the new customer. Is tomorrow at 10.30 OK with you?

Joe

5 Shilpa should

(A) say why she wants to talk to Joe.
(B) tell Joe if she can talk to him tomorrow.
(C) ask the new customer to come to a meeting.

Speaking Part 1

Answer these questions.

- What's your family name?
- How do you spell it?
- Do you work or are you a student?
- What did you do last weekend?

UNIT 2

BEC Preliminary practice

Listening Part 3

2.29

- Look at the notes about a visit to a company that makes different types of food.
- Some information is missing.
- You will hear a manager from the company talking to two members of staff about a visit by new customers.
- For each question 1–7, fill in the missing information in the numbered space using one or two words.
- You will hear the recording twice.

Programme for visit by new customers

Visitors' companies are (1) ______________________ in Switzerland, France, etc.

Day: next (2) ______________________ (13 July)

Timetable:

10am: meet the visitors in reception area of (3) ______________________ office
Coffee in room 106
Talk by Joanna, the (4) ______________________ Manager, about:
- company history
- new (5) ______________________ (curry sauces and frozen pizzas)

11am: tour of the (6) ______________________

12.30pm: lunch in canteen

After lunch: Tom, the Customer (7) ______________________ Manager, will talk to them

3pm: end of visit

Writing Part 1

- You need a new administrative assistant in your department.
- Write an email to your company's Human Resources department:
  - asking them to advertise for an administrative assistant
  - telling them when you want the new person to start work
  - saying what the new person's working hours will be.
- Write between 30 and 40 words.
- Do not write in capital letters.

UNIT 3 BEC Preliminary practice

Reading Part 4

- Read the magazine article below about a company called Marshall & Picton.
- Are sentences 1–7 below 'Right' or 'Wrong'? If there is not enough information to answer 'Right' or 'Wrong', choose 'Doesn't say'.
- For each sentence (1–7), mark one letter (A, B or C).

Marshall & Picton

Marshall & Picton is a company that makes many different pharmaceutical products. Its head office is in Cardiff, the capital city of Wales.

The company has nearly 200 employees – a third at its head office and the others in its two research and development laboratories. Most employees work full-time, but some work part-time.

The company sells most of its products through pharmacies in the UK, but it also exports some of them, mostly to countries in western Europe.

The Chief Executive of Marshall & Picton is Stephen Marshall. His grandfather started Marshall's as a pharmaceutical company in 1924, with its head office in Bristol, England. In 1936 it joined another company in the same industry, Picton's. That was when Marshall & Picton was established. The company moved to Cardiff in 2004.

Stephen Marshall joined the company as an administrative assistant when he left school, and he became Chief Executive 15 years ago. His daughter Amanda also works for the company, as a product planner.

1 Marshall & Picton is a pharmaceutical company.

(A) Right (B) Wrong (C) Doesn't say

2 The company has more than 200 employees.

(A) Right (B) Wrong (C) Doesn't say

3 The part-time staff work in the research and development laboratories.

(A) Right (B) Wrong (C) Doesn't say

4 The company exports most of its products.

(A) Right (B) Wrong (C) Doesn't say

5 Picton's was a pharmaceutical company before it joined Marshall's.

(A) Right (B) Wrong (C) Doesn't say

6 Marshall & Picton was established in 1936.

(A) Right (B) Wrong (C) Doesn't say

7 Amanda Marshall joined Marshall & Picton when she left school.

(A) Right (B) Wrong (C) Doesn't say

Speaking Part 2

Give a short presentation on this topic for about a minute. You will have a minute to prepare this and you can make notes if you want.

What is important when establishing a new company

- Type of products
- Location
- Number of employees

Now answer these questions.

- Is it important to find out about competition?
- How can a new company find customers?
- Would you like to establish a new company? Why, or why not?

UNIT 4

BEC Preliminary practice

Reading Part 2

- Look at the list below. It shows some jobs.
- For questions 1–5, decide which job (A–H) would be suitable for each person.
- For each question, mark one letter (A–H).
- Do not use any letter more than once.

Jobs

A Accountant
B Administrative assistant
C Pharmacist
D Researcher
E Sales assistant
F Service engineer
G Software designer
H Tour guide

1 ☐ Sally wants to take groups of visitors round historic cities.

2 ☐ Walid hopes to work in an office, where he can arrange meetings and type letters.

3 ☐ Gaby would like to work in a shop and sell clothes to customers.

4 ☐ Lucia wants a job where she keeps records of the money that goes in and out of a company.

5 ☐ Martin is looking for a job where he makes sure that machines are working correctly.

Writing Part 2

- Read this part of a letter from Julia Simmons.

> I am taking a two-year IT course at college, which will end next month. I am very interested in designing websites and software, and would like to work for your company's IT department. Would it be possible to come and talk to you about jobs, please?
>
> Many thanks
>
> Julia Simmons

- Write a letter to Ms Simmons:
  - thanking her for her letter
  - suggesting that she applies for a job with your company as a web designer
  - saying how she should apply
  - suggesting when she can come and talk to you.
- Write 60–80 words.
- Do not include any postal addresses.

Dear Ms Simmons

UNIT 5 BEC Preliminary practice

Listening Part 1

2.30–2.37

- For questions 1–8, you will hear eight short recordings.
- For each question, mark one letter (A, B or C) for the correct answer.

Example

Where will Frank take the new employees first?

(A) Research & Development (B) Human Resources (C) Marketing

The answer is C.

- You will hear the eight recordings twice.

1 When does David leave work most days?

(A) 17:00 (B) 17:30 (C) 18:00

2 Where is Carol Lorimer?

(A) in a meeting
(B) on a business trip
(C) in her office

3 Which restaurant will they take the customer to?

(A) THE AMAZON

(B) Tommy's

(C) The Golden Palace

4 Which product's sales are higher than last month?

(A)  (B)  (C) 

5 Which chart shows the company's employees this year?

(A) 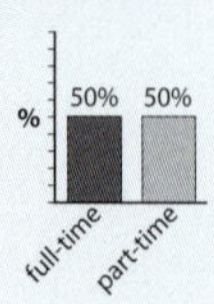

(B) 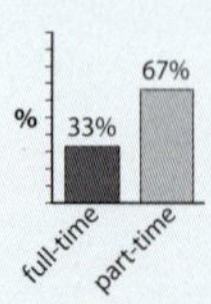

(C) 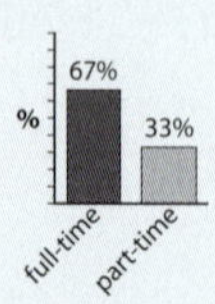

6 What does the caller want Barry to do?

(A) send him an email
(B) meet him
(C) call him back

7 How did Maggie travel to Edinburgh?

(A)  (B) 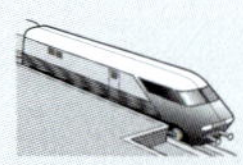 (C) 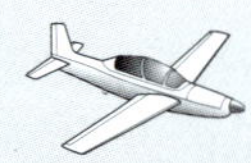

8 Which web design company will they use?

(A) COMPUTER DREAMS

(B) GGT

(C) Charlton Web

Speaking Part 1

Answer these questions.

- Do you ever phone companies?
- Is it easier to phone a company or send an email to them?
- Do you think companies should provide training for staff who answer the phone?
- Would you like to have a job where you answer the phone a lot?

UNIT 6

BEC Preliminary practice

Reading Part 5

- Read the article below about a successful businesswoman.
- For each questions 1–6, choose the correct answer.
- Mark one letter (A, B or C).

DR's: a very successful small clothing business

Donna Reed has always enjoyed designing and making clothes for herself. A few years ago she thought about doing it as a business. But there were lots of designers of women's clothing, and she knew it would be too difficult to sell her clothes. She wasn't very interested in children's clothes, so she decided to make men's clothing.

Donna started looking for a suitable place to work. She needed an office and a workroom for making the clothes. She wanted it to be near her home. Most of the places she looked at were too expensive, but after six months she found somewhere suitable. It was cheap, and big enough, but it was a long way from her home. So she bought a car.

Donna then started her business, which she called DR's. Her plan was to design and make all the clothes herself. She did the marketing by spending two days a week visiting clothes shops and trying to persuade them to sell her clothes. And she employed a part-time accountant to look after the finances of the business.

It was difficult to find customers. Most shops liked her designs, but didn't have enough room for her clothing. So Donna decided to start advertising. Advertising on television was too expensive, so she advertised in some family magazines, because she thought their readers would be interested in her products. She also thought about advertising on the internet, but decided not to.

Sales increased a little, but not enough. So Donna opened a shop, which would sell only the clothes she designed and made. She rented a shop close to her office, and employed some shop assistants. At first there were only a few customers, but they recommended the shop to their friends, and more and more customers came in. After six months the shop was very busy, and selling lots of clothes.

The business is now very successful, and Donna wants it to grow. She plans to open two more shops in the next twelve months. People have suggested that she tries exporting her clothes, but she thinks it would be too difficult. Donna is now so busy that it will be a long time before she stops working!

1 What did Donna decide to make?
- (A) men's clothes
- (B) women's clothes
- (C) children's clothes

2 What was the problem with the place where Donna set up her business?
- (A) It was too small.
- (B) It was expensive.
- (C) It was far from her home.

3 The first person Donna employed was
- (A) a marketing assistant
- (B) a clothes designer
- (C) an accountant

4 Where did Donna advertise at first?
- (A) on TV
- (B) in magazines
- (C) on the internet

5 During the shop's first six months, the number of customers
- (A) rose.
- (B) fell.
- (C) stayed the same.

6 What is Donna planning to do next?
- (A) export her clothes
- (B) open more shops
- (C) stop working

Speaking Part 3B

Answer these questions about selling clothes.

- How important is it for a clothes manufacturer to advertise?
- How can clothes manufacturers find out what customers want to buy?
- Should a company that makes clothes have its own shops?
- Is it important for customers who buy clothes to know the name of the manufacturer?

UNIT 7

BEC Preliminary practice

Speaking Part 3

Situation

A company makes sports equipment and sells it to sports centres in countries around the world. The company wants to find out what its customers think of its products. Talk together for about two minutes about some of the ways that the company could contact its customers, and decide together which 3 ways would be most useful.

Here are some ideas to help you.

- Ways of contacting customers
- Telephone call
- Text message
- Email
- Voicemail
- Written questionnaire
- Video conference
- Face-to-face meeting

Now answer these questions.

- How important is it for a company to find out what customers think of its products?
- Should a company ask its customers what new products to make?
- How often do you think companies should contact their business customers?
- Do you think retailers should contact their customers?

Writing Part 1

- You want to arrange to meet somebody who works in a different part of your company.
- Write an email to the person:
  - explaining why you want to meet them
  - suggesting a date when you are free
  - inviting them to come to your office for the meeting.
- Write 30–40 words.
- Do not write in capital letters.

UNIT 8

BEC Preliminary practice

Reading Part 6

- Read the letter below.
- Choose the correct word to fill each gap from A, B or C.
- For each question 1–12, mark one letter (A, B or C).

Dear Ms Shillingford

Position of Marketing Manager

Thank you very **(1)** ___________ for your application for this position. I **(2)** ___________ pleased to invite you to come to the company on September 12th **(3)** ___________ 10.30 a.m. This will **(4)** ___________ an informal meeting with some of the staff of the marketing **(5)** ___________

When you arrive at the main entrance, please go first to Reception, where you will **(6)** ___________ to sign in. Then please come to the Johnson Room. **(7)** ___________ is a lift in **(8)** ___________ corner of the Reception area. Take the lift to the second floor – be careful, because it **(9)** ___________ stop at the first floor. When you go out of the lift, **(10)** ___________ right. The Johnson Room is the **(11)** ___________ room on the left, **(12)** ___________ to the stairs.

I look forward to seeing you on the 12th.

Yours sincerely

Bob Gifford

Director of Human Resources

1	(A) most	(B) much	(C) many
2	(A) am	(B) is	(C) are
3	(A) on	(B) in	(C) at
4	(A) have	(B) do	(C) be
5	(A) department	(B) factory	(C) cafeteria
6	(A) ought	(B) must	(C) need
7	(A) There	(B) It	(C) Where
8	(A) the	(B) any	(C) both
9	(A) don't	(B) didn't	(C) doesn't
10	(A) run	(B) turn	(C) walk
11	(A) late	(B) last	(C) latest
12	(A) next	(B) beside	(C) across

Writing Part 2

Read the part of a letter below from David Bowyer, the Head of Business Studies at your local college.

> I am writing to ask whether it will be possible for the college's first year business students to visit your company. It would be very useful for them to spend a morning learning about the different parts of your business, and hearing about people's jobs. There will be a maximum of 20 students.

- Write a letter to Mr Bowyer:
  - thanking him for his letter
  - suggesting when the students can visit your company
  - offering to introduce the students to some of your staff
  - saying what parts of the company they will see.
- Write 60–80 words.
- Do not include any postal addresses.

Dear Mr Bowyer

UNIT 9

BEC Preliminary practice

Listening Part 4

2.38

- You will hear an interview on a local radio station with Gerald Seymour, the Chief Executive of a company that has just moved into the town.
- For each question 1–8, mark one letter (A, B or C) for the correct answer.
- You will hear the interview twice.

1 The company was established in Chorley to be close to

(A) suppliers.
(B) workers.
(C) retailers.

2 The Chorley factory is

(A) bigger than the old factory.
(B) smaller than the old factory.
(C) the same size as the old factory.

3 Who suggested moving to Chorley?

(A) the Finance Director
(B) the Production Director
(C) the Human Resources Director

4 Who planned the move to Chorley?

(A) the board of directors
(B) a team of three people
(C) the warehouse manager

5 How long has the company been in Chorley?

(A) three weeks
(B) nine months
(C) a year

6 What is the company going to start making?

(A) boxes of chocolates
(B) drinking chocolate
(C) chocolate bars

7 What does Gerald Seymour like most about Chorley?

(A) the nearby countryside
(B) the entertainments
(C) the shops

8 How often does Gerald eat chocolate?

(A) every day
(B) once a week
(C) once a month

Speaking Part 2

Give a short presentation on this topic for about a minute. You will have a minute to prepare this and you can make notes if you want.

What is important when?

looking for a new job

- Job advertisements
- Company websites
- Advice from friends

Now answer these questions.

- How important is the salary?
- Is it a good idea to apply for lots of jobs?
- How can you prepare for a job interview?

UNIT 10 BEC Preliminary practice

Reading Part 3

- Look at the chart below. It shows the profits of two companies over an eight-year period.
- Which year does each sentence (1–5) describe?
- For each sentence, mark one letter (A–H).
- Do not use any letter more than once.

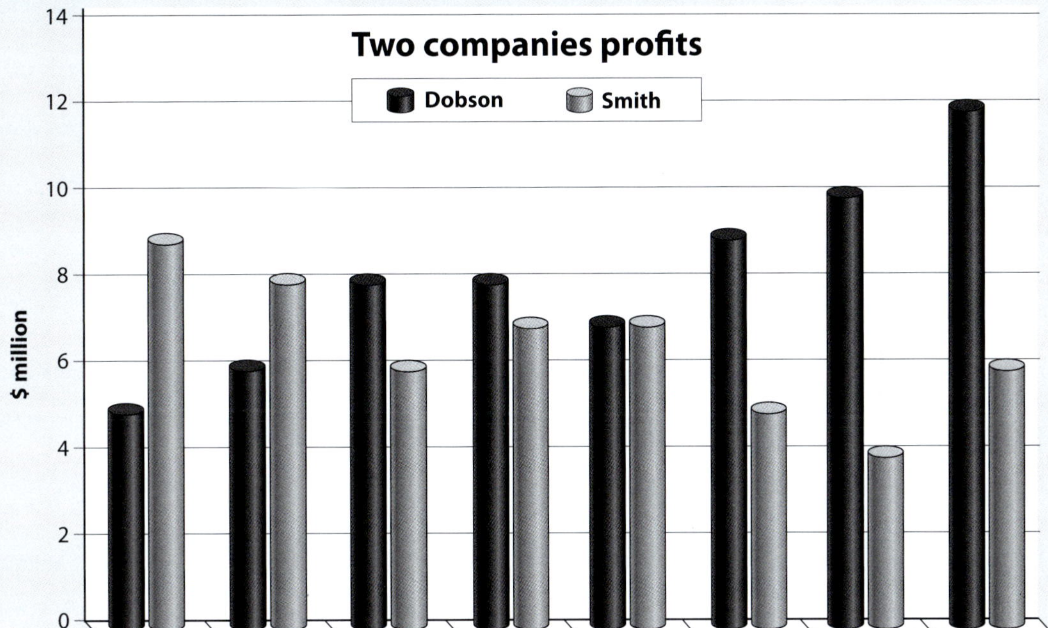

	A	B	C	D	E	F	G	H
Dobson	5	6	8	8	7	9	10	12
Smith	9	8	6	7	7	5	4	6

Year

1 In this year, Dobson's profits rose but remained lower than Smith's profits.

2 Dobson's profits continued to increase in this year, while Smith's profits reached their lowest level.

3 Dobson's profits were lower this year than the year before, and were the same as Smith's profits.

4 In this year Smith's profits fell below the level of Dobson's profits for the first time.

5 Smith's profits rose this year after a fall the year before, while Dobson's profits reached their highest level.

Writing Part 1

- You want your Assistant to give a presentation to some customers.
- Write an email to your assistant:
  - asking him to give the presentation
  - telling him when the presentation will take place
  - saying why you can't give the presentation yourself.
- Write 30–40 words.
- Do not write in capital letters.

UNIT 11

BEC Preliminary practice

Reading Part 7

- Read the two emails below.
- Complete the booking form below.
- Write a word or phrase (in CAPITAL LETTERS) or a number on lines 1–5.

To: Janet Flowers
From: Henry Grant
Subject: Marketing conference

Hi Janet

I've received the email below from Galliford Training. I'd like you to attend the second conference. It's easier to travel from here to Glasgow than to Edinburgh, so book the session there. You should also request a parking space.

Henry

-----Original message-----

To: Henry Grant, BGT Ltd

From: Marianne@GallifordTraining

Subject: Marketing conferences

If you work in marketing, we can help you to improve your company's sales figures. We run one-day conferences. Here are the next two:

15 April, 9.30-4.30, Glasgow and Edinburgh. Direct Marketing
22 May, 9.30-4.30, Glasgow and Edinburgh. Using Social Media

For further information and to book a place, contact Keith Francis.

GALLIFORD TRAINING *Conference booking form*

Full name of person attending conference:	**(1)**
Name of company:	**(2)**
Date of conference:	**(3)**
Place of conference:	**(4)**
Any requirement(s):	needs a **(5)**

Speaking Part 3B

Answer these questions about company plans.

- Should a company consult all its employees about its plans?
- Should plans be written down?
- Do you think companies should ever change their plans?
- How important is it for a company to get advice from consultants about its plans?

UNIT 12

BEC Preliminary practice

Listening Part 2

2.39

- Look at the notes below.
- Some information is missing.
- You will hear a man telephoning a catering company to order lunch for a meeting.
- For each question 1–7, fill in the missing information in the numbered space using a word, numbers or letters.
- You will hear the conversation twice.

Honeyfresh Catering Order form

Contact name:	*John* **(1)**
Company:	*Rathbone Engineering*
Address:	*Unit* **(2)** , *Frankland Business Park*
Phone number:	**(3)**
Meal:	*Buffet lunch*
Date:	**(4)** *June*
Time:	**(5)**
Number of people:	**(6)**
Cost:	**(7)** *£* *per person*

Writing Part 2

Read the part of an email from Honeyfresh Catering below.

To:
From: s.fielding
Subject: Lunch

Thank you for ordering a buffet lunch from Honeyfresh Catering. I hope that your company was satisfied with the meal we provided for you last week. Would you please tell me what you thought of the food, and of our catering staff.

I hope we will be able to work together again in the future.

Regards

Sonia Fielding

Managing Director

- Write an email to Sonia Fielding:
  - thanking her for providing the lunch
  - answering her question about the food
  - mentioning the friendliness of her staff
  - asking for the invoice.
- Write 60–80 words.
- Do not include any addresses.

To:
From:
Subject:

Dear Ms Fielding

Wordlist

(n) = noun   *(v)* = verb   *(adj)* = adjective   *(adv)* = adverb

Unit 1

accountant *(n)*
administrative assistant *(n)*
advertising *(n)*
area code *(n)*
business card *(n)*
construction *(n)*
conversation *(n)*
country code *(n)*
department *(n)*
designer *(n)*
dot *(n)*
email *(v)*
engineer *(n)*
human resources *(n)*
imaginary *(adj)*
information technology *(n)*
limited *(adj)*
logo *(n)*
manager *(n)*
marketing *(n)*
meet *(v)*
planner *(n)*
post code *(n)*
pretend *(v)*
product *(n)*
purchase *(v)*
researcher *(n)*
sales assistant *(n)*
underscore *(v)*
zip code *(n)*

Unit 2

customer *(n)*
manufacturing *(n)*
married *(adj)*
meeting *(n)*
muffin *(n)*
pass *(n)*
presentation *(n)*
sandwich *(n)*
schedule *(n)*
support *(n)*
teleconference *(n)*
train *(n)*

Unit 3

build *(v)*
design *(v)*
develop *(v)*
employee *(n)*
establish *(v)*
full-time *(adj)*
integrated circuit *(n)*
produce *(v)*
provide *(v)*

Unit 4

advice *(n)*
angry *(adj)*
boring *(adj)*
confusing *(adj)*
corporate *(adj)*
culture *(n)*
custom *(n)*
difficult *(adj)*
earlier *(adj)*
exhausted *(adj)*
frustrating *(adj)*
hiking *(n)*
impolite *(adj)*
manual *(n)*
miss *(v)*
online *(adj)*
paint *(v)*
polite *(adj)*
pretty *(adv)*
situation *(n)*
sleepy *(adj)*
small talk *(n)*
tone *(n)*
training *(n)*

Unit 5

finance *(n)*
message *(n)*
receptionist *(n)*
text message *(n)*
transfer *(v)*

Unit 6

compact *(adj)*
discount *(n)*
display *(v)*
efficient *(adj)*
energy *(n)*
expensive *(adj)*
fashionable *(adj)*
heavy *(adj)*
ladder *(n)*
light *(adj)*
mailing *(n)*
package *(n)*
smartphone *(n)*
promise *(v)*
quality *(n)*
refreshing *(adj)*
reliable *(adj)*
scooter *(n)*
script *(n)*
shredder *(n)*
smartphone *(n)*
worse *(adj)*

Unit 7

chat *(v)*
complicated *(adj)*
formal *(adj)*
efficient *(adj)*
inefficient *(adj)*
informal *(adj)*
quantity *(n)*
reservation *(n)*
simple *(adj)*

Unit 8

cash machine *(n)*
cosmetics [plural] *(n)*
drinking fountain *(n)*
furniture *(n)*
hall *(n)*
lift *(n)*
personal assistant *(n)*

Unit 9

curriculum vitae (CV) *(n)*
data *(n)*
delivery *(n)*
feedback *(n)*
flow chart *(n)*
inventory *(n)*
invoice *(n)*
launch *(v)*
layout *(n)*
professional *(adj)*
recruit *(v)*
shy *(adj)*
smoothie *(n)*
strength *(n)*
turn off *(phrasal verb)*
weakness *(n)*

Unit 10

audience *(n)*
atmosphere *(n)*
average *(adj)*
bar graph *(n)*
budget *(n)*
complaint *(n)*
decrease *(v)*
distracting *(adj)*
increase *(v)*
invent *(v)*
joke *(v)*
joke *(n)*
official *(adj)*
pie chart *(n)*
population *(n)*
prime minister *(n)*
sharply *(adv)*
slightly *(adv)*
topic *(n)*
visual aid *(n)*

Unit 11

agenda *(n)*
contract *(n)*
cost *(n)*
estimate *(n)*
expand *(v)*
hire *(v)*
marathon *(n)*
next *(adj)*
overseas *(adv)*
send *(v)*
step *(n)*

Unit 12

accessory *(n)*
allergic *(adj)*
brownie *(n)*
chopstick *(n)*
compliment *(n)*
dip *(v)*
impression *(n)*
hurt (someone's feelings) *(v)*
diet *(n)*
recipe *(n)*
salty *(adj)*
shrimp *(n)*
spicy *(adj)*
vanilla *(n)*
vegetarian *(adj)*

Look it Up

MACMILLAN DICTIONARY
Search
Dictionary Thesaurus
www.macmillandictionary.com

These words are all on the Viewpoints pages and the definitions are taken from the *Macmillan English Dictionary* second edition.

All red words have a 'star rating':

★★★ the 2,500 most common and basic English words

★★ very common words

★ fairly common words

Unit 1

fancy (*adj*) ★
not plain or simple but with a lot of decorations or extra parts

organize (*v*) ★★★
to put things into a sensible order or into a system in which all parts work well together

plain (*adj*) ★★
simple in design, with no decoration

pocket (*n*) ★★★
a small bag that forms part of a piece of clothing and is used for holding small objects

receive (*v*) ★★★
to get something that someone gives or sends to you

respect (*n*) ★★★
a feeling that something is important and deserves serious attention

Unit 2

flexitime (*n*)
a system in which workers choose the hours each day that they work, as long as the hours add up to the same fixed number of hours every week or month

(*American* **flextime**)

holiday (*n*) ★★★
the number of days or weeks during a year when you do not have to work but are paid.

(*American* **vacation**)

overtime (*n*) ★
extra hours that someone works at their job

property developer (*n*)
someone who earns money by buying land and building on it

telecommuter (*n*)
someone who works from home on a computer and sends work to their office over telephone lines by MODEM or FAX

time off (*n*)
time when you are not at work or at school

Unit 3

automotive (*adj*)
relating to cars

banking (*n*) ★★
the work done by banks and other financial institutions

chemical (*adj*) ★★
involving chemistry or produced by a method used in chemistry

education (*n*) ★★★
the activity of educating people in schools, colleges, and universities, and all the policies and arrangements concerning this

electronics (*n*) ★★
the science and technology that uses or produces electronic equipment

entertainment (*n*) ★★
performances that people enjoy

farming (*n*) ★
the activity or business of being a farmer

fishing (*n*) ★★
the sport or business of catching fish

health care (*n*) ★★
the services that look after people's health

hospitality (*n*) ★
food, drink, and entertainment given to customers by a company or organization

IT (*n*) ★
information technology: the use of computers and other electronic equipment to store, process, and send information

the media (*n*) ★★★
radio, television, newspapers, the internet, and magazines considered as a group: can be followed by a singular or plural verb

mining (*n*) ★
the process of getting coal or metal from under the ground

news (*n*) ★★★
information about recent events that is reported in newspapers or on television or radio

pharmaceutical (*adj*)
relating to the production or sale of medicines and drugs used for treating medical conditions

software *(n)* ★★★
programs used by computers for doing particular jobs

tourism *(n)* ★★
the business of providing services for people who are travelling for their holiday

transportation *(n)* ★
the activity of moving people or things from one place to another, or the system used for doing this

Unit 4

casual *(adj)* ★★
relaxed and informal

greet *(v)* ★★
to behave in a polite or friendly way towards someone when you meet them

manners [plural] *(n)* ★★★
traditionally accepted ways of behaving that show a polite respect for other people

opinion *(n)* ★★★
the attitude that you have towards something, especially your thoughts about how good it is

praise *(v)* ★★
to express strong approval or admiration for someone or something, especially in public

Unit 5

alarm *(n)* ★★
(an alarm clock: a clock that wakes you up at a particular time by making a noise)

convenient *(adj)* ★★
easy to do, or not causing problems or difficulties

text *(v)*
to send a written message to someone using a mobile phone

(***American*** **cell phone**)

text message *(n)*
A written message that you send or receive using a mobile phone

Unit 6

annoyed *(adj)* ★★
feeling slightly angry or impatient

bother *(v)* ★★★
if you do not bother to do something, you do not do it, either because there seems to be no good reason or because it involves too much effort

celebrity *(n)* ★
a famous person, especially in entertainment or sport

competitor *(n)* ★★
a company that sells the same goods or services as another company

endorsement *(n)*
an occasion when someone famous says in an advertisement that they like a product

especially *(adv)* ★★★
used when mentioning conditions that make something more relevant, important, or true

flash *(v)* ★★
to shine brightly for a very short time, or to shine on and off very quickly

image *(n)* ★★★
a photograph, painting, or other work of art that represents a person or thing

interrupt *(v)* ★★
to make something stop for a period of time

Unit 7

chat *(v)* ★★
to exchange messages with someone using a computer so that you are able to see each other's messages immediately, especially on the internet

complicated *(adj)* ★★
difficult to do, deal with, or understand, especially because of involving a lot of different processes or aspects

formal *(adj)* ★★★
following the correct or suitable official methods

efficient *(adj)* ★★★
something that is efficient works well and produces good results by using the available time, money, supplies etc in the most effective way

inefficient *(adj)*
not working in the best possible way, especially by not using time, supplies, energy etc in the most effective way

informal *(adj)* ★★
relaxed and friendly

simple *(adj)* ★★★
easy to understand, solve, or do

teleconference *(n)*
a meeting held among people in different places using an electronic communications system, often television

Unit 8

chemist *(n)* ★★
a shop that sells medicines, beauty products and toiletries

clinic *(n)* ★★
a place where people go to receive a particular type of medical treatment or advice

convenience store *(n)*
a small shop that is open for long hours and sells a variety of goods, especially food and drink, cleaning materials, and newspapers or magazines

facility *(n)* ★★★
something such as a room or piece of equipment that is provided at a place for people to use

flexible *(adj)* ★★
able to make changes or deal with a situation that is changing

insurance *(n)* ★★★
an arrangement in which you regularly pay an **insurance company** an amount of money so that they will give you money if something you own is damaged, lost, or stolen, or if you die or are ill or injured

laundry *(n)* ★
a business that washes and irons clothes

shift *(n)* ★★
a period of work time in a factory, hospital, or other place where some people work during the day and some work at night

vending machine *(n)*
a machine that you can buy things from, for example cigarettes, sweets, or drinks

(***American*** **candy**)

yoga *(n)*
an activity that involves doing physical and breathing exercises to make you stronger and make your mind and body relax

Unit 9

graduate *(v)* ★
to complete your studies at a university or college, usually by getting a **degree**

internship *(n)*
a job that a student or someone who has recently obtained a degree takes in order to get experience

recommend *(v)* ★★★
to say that someone or something is good and worth using, having, or experiencing

Unit 10

slide *(n)* ★★
a small piece of film in a frame, that you shine light through in order to show the image on a screen

Unit 11

continue *(v)* ★★★
to keep doing something without stopping

Unit 12

appreciate *(v)* ★★
to recognize the good or special qualities of a person, place, or thing

communal *(adj)* ★
owned or used by everyone in a group, especially a group of people who live in the same building

entertain *(v)* ★★
to receive someone as a guest and give them food and drink or other forms of enjoyment

left-handed *(adj)*
someone who is left-handed is born with a natural tendency to use their left hand to do things, especially things such as writing

social *(adj)* ★★★
relating to activities that involve being with other people, especially activities that you do for pleasure

traditional *(adj)* ★★★
relating to or based on very old customs, beliefs, or stories

Common irregular verbs

Here is a list of common irregular verbs in English with their past tense (*I* ***took*** *the test*) and past participle (*I have* ***taken*** *three tests this month*).

Base form	Simple past	Past participle
be	was/were	been
become	became	become
begin	began	begun
break	broke	broken
bring	brought	brought
buy	bought	bought
catch	caught	caught
choose	chose	chosen
come	came	come
cost	cost	cost
cut	cut	cut
do	did	done
draw	drew	drawn
drink	drank	drunk
drive	drove	driven
eat	ate	eaten
fall	fell	fallen
feel	felt	felt
find	found	found
fly	flew	flown
forget	forgot	forgotten
get	got	got
give	gave	given
go	went	gone
have	had	had
hear	heard	heard
know	knew	known
leave	left	left
lose	lost	lost

Base form	Simple past	Past participle
make	made	made
meet	met	met
pay	paid	paid
put	put	put
read	read	read
ride	rode	ridden
run	ran	run
say	said	said
see	saw	seen
sell	sold	sold
send	sent	sent
show	showed	shown
sing	sang	sung
sit	sat	sat
sleep	slept	slept
speak	spoke	spoken
spend	spent	spent
stand	stood	stood
swim	swam	swum
take	took	taken
teach	taught	taught
tell	told	told
think	thought	thought
throw	threw	thrown
understand	understood	understood
wear	wore	worn
win	won	won
write	wrote	written

UNIT 1 Grammar reference

The verb *to be*

Use the verb *to be* to give your name, your job, and say what company you're with. Contractions are more common in speech.

Long form	Contractions
I am with Globaltech. I am not with Eurofund.	I'm with Globaltech. I'm not with Eurofund.
You / we / they are in Advertising. You / we / they are not in Sales.	You're / we're / they're in Advertising. You're / we're / they're not in Sales. You / we / they aren't in Sales.
He / she is a Marketing Assistant. He / she is not a Manager.	He's / she's a Marketing Assistant. He's / she's not a Manager. He / she isn't a Manager.

The present simple statements

Use the present simple to talk about facts and habits.

Subject	Regular verbs
I / you / we / they	work, live, start, give, leave meet, like, make
He / she / it	works, lives, starts, gives, leaves, meets, likes, makes

I work for IWT.

She gives her business card to lots of people.

My train leaves in an hour.

Practice the verb *to be*

1 Complete the paragraph with words from the box. One word is not used.

aren't is isn't	m m not	re s

Nice to meet you. 1) I'______ Shelly Silver. I work for Immedia. 2) We'______ a global technology company. 3) I usually work at the head office – that'______ in Munich. 4) I'______ there now because I'm in Moscow for three weeks to visit our branch office. 5) Here ______ my card. If you want to meet later, please get in touch. 6) But my mobile phone ______ working here, so please use my email.

2 Write the correct form of *to be*.

1 Mr Kahn __________ from Germany. He's from Austria.

2 A: __________ you Canadian?
B: Yes, I am.

3 A: __________ this your business card?
B: No, it __________ .

4 My coworkers and I __________ late today.

5 __________ she new here?

6 I __________ with Lake & Bowen.

7 A: Sorry, am I late?
B: No, you __________ .

8 I'm looking for Maria and Carlo, but they __________ here.

Practice the present simple – statements

3 Answer the questions.

1 Do you live in Zurich? *No I live in Stuttgart.*

2 Who do you work for? ______________________

3 Where do you live? ______________________

4 What does your company make? ______________________

5 Who do you give your business cards to?

____

UNIT 2

Grammar reference

Prepositions of time *at/on/in*

Use **at** with the time of day, with some expressions for part of the day and with special times of the year.

at	2 o'clock, 11:30, half past 6, midnight lunchtime, night Hanukkah, Easter, Eid ul-Fitr

Use **on** with dates, with days of the week and with special holidays. Note, we write '15th May' but we say 'the 15th of May'.

on	15th May, Tuesday, Monday afternoon Mother's Day, New Year's Eve

Use **in** with months, years, seasons and parts of the day

in	July, November, 1955, 2014 winter, autumn, spring the afternoon, the evening

Do not use ***at/on/in*** with ***next/last/every.***

I have a job interview next Tuesday.

We visited China last December.

I go to the gym every evening.

Practice prepositions of time – *at/on/in*

1 Complete the sentences with *at*, *on* or *in*.

1 ______ March Hiro Makino went to the US. He left Shanghai ______ 15th March and he arrived in New York ______ 7:00pm.

2 In Japan, new employees usually join their companies ______ spring.

3 The meeting is ______ Thursday ______ half past 4. ______ the evening there will be a welcome party.

4 Michel DuBois was born ______ Christmas Day, 1989.

2 Danielle is telling her mother about her week. Complete the description by using *at*, *on*, *in* or *nothing* (–).

'Hi Mum, how was your week? ______ last week I was so busy! I know I say that ______ every week, but this time it's true! ______ Monday I had to work late, I finished ______ 11:00pm and had to take a taxi home. I know, we're always busy ______ autumn, but my boss says that ______ next year we'll employ some more staff, so I hope I can take a holiday ______ June. Anyway, ______ next weekend I'll come home so I'll see you ______ Friday night – the train leaves here ______ 7 o'clock and I'll arrive there ______ 10 ______ the evening. Can you pick me up at the station?'

UNIT 3

Grammar reference

Questions and answers with *do* and *does*

Yes/no questions

Questions that can be answered with *yes* or *no* are formed by putting *do* or *does* before the subject and the main verb.

Statement	Question
I / you / we / they work for a design company.	Do I / you / we / they work for a design company?
He /she lives in Budapest.	Does he /she live in Budapest?

Note: questions can be answered with short answers (*Yes, I do.; No, he doesn't.*), but also with additional information (*Q: Does this bus run in the morning? A: There's one at 9:00.*).

Information questions *(what, where, when, why, how, how much/often)*

Form information questions with the question word first, then *do* or *does*, and then the subject and main verb.

How many employees do you have?
Where do we eat lunch?
What company does he work for?
How often does she work late?

Practice: questions and answers with *do* and *does*

1 Write the words in the correct order to make questions.

1 do / offices / you / how / have / many ?

______

2 export / does / goods / your company ?

______

3 your / you / job / like / do ?

______

4 to work / in / your friend / does / Tourism / want ?

______

5 do / does / what / company / your ?

______

6 time / you / what / work / do / finish ?

______

2 Match the questions in Practice 1 to the answers a–g. There is one extra answer.

a We design posters and brochures. ______
b Yes, I love it. ______
c Three – two in Germany and one in France. ______
d Usually around six. ______
e We have around 2,300 employees. ______
f Not really. He's looking for a job in Sales. ______
g No, we don't. We only import them. ______

UNIT 4

Grammar reference

Short responses – *Me too / So do I / Really? / Neither can I*

Use short responses to show agreement or disagreement, to show similar experiences or feelings and to keep the conversation going. The form of the auxiliary verb should match the statement it refers to.

I **love** Chinese food.	So **do** I.	I **don't**.
I'**m** angry with my boss.	So **am** I.	I'**m** not.
I **watched** TV last night.	So **did** I.	I **didn't**.
My boss **was** late to work today.	So **was** I.	I **wasn't**.
My sister **can** play the violin.	So **can** I.	I **can't**.

Where the main statement is negative, use *neither* in place of *so*.

I **can't** use this new software.	Neither **can** I.	I **can**.
I **don't** like long meetings.	Neither **do** I.	I **do**.
I'**ve** never seen Star Wars.	Neither **have** I.	I **have**.

Should (Why don't you...?) and *recommend (How about...?)*

Use *should, why don't you, recommend* or *how about* to give advice or make a suggestion. Use the base form with *should* and *why don't you*. Use the present participle (*-ing*) with *recommend* and *how about*.

You should join a gym.	I recommend asking for a raise.
Why don't you join a gym?	How about asking for a raise?

Practice: short responses – *Me too / So do I / Really? / Neither can I*

1 Respond to Tina's statements with information about yourself.

	Tina	You
1	'I don't have his phone number.'	'Don't you? ______________________.'
2	'I have a bad cold.'	'Do you? ______________________.'
3	'I worked hard this morning.'	'Did you? ______________________.'
4	'I've never been to the US.'	'Haven't you? ______________________.'
5	'I can't play mahjong.'	'Can't you? ______________________.'

Practice: *Should (Why don't you...?)* and *recommend (How about...?)*

2 Write some advice to your friend.

1 You talk too fast. ______________________

2 Your hair is too long. ______________________

3 You look tired. ______________________

4 You look hungry. ______________________

UNIT 5 Grammar reference

Can for permission and requests

Use *can* to request information or ask for permission to do something.

Note: Some people use *may* in more formal situations.

Can (May) I speak to Mr Smith? / Can (May) I open the window?

Use *can* to politely ask someone to do something.

Note: We don't use *may* in these situations.

Can you sit here, please? / Can you say that again?

Do not confuse these situations with using *can* for ability:

Can you speak Polish?

Practice: *can* for permission and requests

1 Circle the appropriate response.

1 Can you say your name again, please?
   a Yes, I can.
   b Geeta Singh.

2 Can I speak to the Manager?
   a I'm sorry, he's not here right now.
   b Certainly. Please tell him I called.

3 Can I take a message?
   a No, thank you.
   b No, you can't.

4 Can you use this software?
   a I'm on a business trip.
   b Yes, I can.

5 Can I see you on Tuesday?
   a I'll transfer your call.
   b I'm sorry, I'm busy then.

2 Match the situations 1–5 to the appropriate questions a–e.

1 The person you are speaking to is speaking very fast. ______
2 You want to tell Ms Anton something, but she's not there. ______
3 You don't know who is on the phone. ______
4 You don't know how to write someone's name. ______
5 Someone wants to tell your Manager something, but he's not here. ______

a Can I leave a message?
b Can I take a message?
c Can you spell that for me, please?
d I'm sorry, can you speak more slowly?
e Can I ask who's calling?

UNIT 6

Grammar reference

Comparatives – *faster, more reliable*

Use these basic rules to form comparative adjectives.

Short words (one syllable)	add *-er* or *-r*	*old* = *old***er**, *safe* = *safe***r**
Short words with consonant-vowel-consonant	double the final consonant and add *-er*	*big* = *big***ger**, *thin* = *thin***ner**
Longer words (two syllables) ending in *-y*	drop the *-y* and add *-ier*	*easy* = *eas***ier**
Longer words (two or more syllables)	use **more**	*challenging* = **more** *challenging*

Note: some adjectives have irregular comparative forms.
good = *better*   *bad* = *worse*   *fun* = *more fun*   *far* = *further*

Practice: comparatives – *faster, more reliable*

1 Make sentences comparing these items. Use the comparative form of the adjectives in brackets.

1 fruit / fried chicken (healthy)
Fruit is healthier than fried chicken.

2 walking / driving (cheap)
____

3 hotels / camping (expensive)
____

4 LEDs / regular light bulbs (efficient)
____

5 bungee jumping / reading a book (exciting)
____

2 Complete Luka's presentation to his customers. Use the correct form of the adjectives in brackets.

'Welcome to our new factory! This facility is ____________ (big), ____________ (modern) and ____________ (energy-efficient) than our other factories. This means we can make products here ____________ (fast) and ____________ (cheap) than before, and with ____________ (good) quality. As a result, we can offer our customers ____________ (short) delivery times and ____________ (few) defects. Let me also say that our workers are ____________ (happy) here – the work is ____________ (safe), working hours are ____________ (short) and the food in the cafeteria is ____________ (delicious)! Now, if you come with me ...'

UNIT 7

Grammar reference

Prepositions – *to* and *about*

Prepositional phrases add more information to a sentence. Use *to* for people and *about* for things.

Can I speak ***to*** *the manager? / I'm calling* ***about*** *my appointment.*

Infinitives

We can use infinitives (*to* + verb) to express purpose. They are often used directly after verbs. Always keep the verb part of the infinitive phrase in the base form.

I'm calling ***to ask*** *about our meeting.*

I'd like ***to confirm*** *the dates.*

Practice: prepositions – *to* and *about*

1 Complete the dialogue with *to* or *about*.

Mr Williams: Hi, can I speak 1) __________ Mr Al Zaidi, please?

Ms Buchieri: Yes, I'll transfer you. Who am I speaking 2) __________?

Mr Williams: Oh, sorry, this is Mr Williams, from Sanyou.

Ms Buchieri: Thank you, Mr Williams. And what is this 3) __________?

Mr Williams: I'm calling 4) __________ the conference next week.

Ms Buchieri: OK, I'll transfer your call … I'm sorry, he's not answering his phone. Would you like to speak 5) __________ his assistant?

Mr Williams: Yes, that's fine. I'm sure she knows 6) __________ the schedule.

Practice: infinitives

2 Complete the sentences with to and one of the words in the box. There is one extra word.

ask	check	listen	make
meet	order	return	

1 I'm trying __________ my email, but it won't open.

2 We'd like __________ coffee and tea for about 240 people.

3 Hi, I'd like __________ a reservation for two for Friday at 6:00.

4 I'm calling __________ if we can meet this week.

5 I need __________ Mr Singh's call.

6 He wants __________ me on Wednesday for a job interview.

UNIT 8

Grammar reference

Imperatives

Use the imperative form for orders, instructions, warnings and suggestions. Depending on the situation and on the intonation and stress, the form can be friendly, angry or neutral. The negative form is usually formed with *Don't (Do not)*.

Warnings	Look out!	Don't touch!
Orders	Follow me.	Come here.
Instructions	Turn left at the corner.	Stay inside the yellow lines.
Suggestions	Don't forget to lock your door.	Try the cafeteria. It's great.

Note: Where something is always true we can use *never* or *always* with the imperative.

Always wear a seatbelt when driving. Never drink and drive.

Practice: imperatives

1 Match 1–8 to a–h to make imperatives.

1	Wait for me	a	the wet paint!
2	Don't touch	b	before you leave the office.
3	Cross the street	c	before meals.
4	Save the document	d	when you enter the aeroplane.
5	Take these pills	e	before you shut down the computer.
6	Push this button	f	at the bus stop.
7	Lock your desk	g	when the light is green.
8	Switch off your phone	h	to transfer the call.

2 Gretchen is giving safety instructions to some visitors to her factory. Complete her speech with the verbs in the box.

follow	keep	put on	stay	
switch off	take	talk	touch	wear

'Good morning, everyone! I'm Gretchen and I'll be your guide inside the mill. Before we start, for your safety there are some rules and instructions I need to go over. First of all, please ____________ these helmets, safety glasses and safety shoes, and to keep your hands clean please ____________ these gloves. When we are in the factory ____________ inside the yellow lines and ____________ your hands out of your pockets. ____________ my instructions at all times and don't ____________ any moving parts. If you have any questions, please ask me – don't ____________ to the operators. Finally, don't ____________ any photographs inside the plant and please ____________ all electronic equipment before we go in. Right, please follow me and I'll show you …'

UNIT 9 Grammar reference

Sequencing words

The words *first*, *second*, *third*, etc., *then* and *finally* almost always come at the beginning of a sentence when you are giving instructions.

First, turn on the printer. Then check the ink levels.

Note: a comma is used after ***first***, ***second***, ***third***, and ***finally***, but not after ***then***.

The words *after (that)* and *next* often come at the beginning of a sentence, but can also come at the end, especially in short sentences.

Next, check the ink levels.

Check the ink levels next.

Note the verb forms required with *before*:

Before turning on *the printer, add the paper.*

Add the paper ***before you turn on*** *the printer.*

Practice: sequencing words

1 Complete the paragraph with words from the box. One word is not used.

after that   before   finally   first   second
then   third

How to use an online storage system

__________, research online to find a storage system you like. Some are free, and some cost money. __________, register for an account. __________, download the software to your computer. Click on the application to open it __________. __________ you upload your files to the online storage folder, make sure you back them up! __________, check to make sure …

2 Write the words in the correct order to make sentences.

1 to / walk / bus stop / first, / the

____

2 number 27 bus / the / second, / to the city centre / take

____

3 the station, / transfer to / get to / the number 12 bus / after you

____

4 you / get off / the big park / the bus before / pass

____

5 minutes after / five / for about / that / walk west

____

6 will see / finally / my house / you

____

UNIT 10

Grammar reference

Past simple

Use the past simple to talk about a situation in the past, an event or events that took place in the past once, several times, or never.

Situation in the past (not true now)	I worked in Germany for 10 years.
Action that finished in the past	Production increased last year.
Series of actions in the past (completed)	I finished the document, saved it and then printed it before the meeting.

For regular verbs, the past simple ends in *-ed* (*work**ed**, play**ed**, manufactur**ed**, graduat**ed**, continu**ed***). Irregular verbs take a different form (*write* = *wrote*, *go* = *went*, *be* = *was* / *were*, *forget* = *forgot*, *take* = *took*, *hear* = *heard*). For a list of common irregular verbs, see page 00.

For questions and negatives, use *did* or *didn't* (with *be* use *was/were*).

Did you call the customer?	Yes, I did.	No, I didn't.
Did you finish the report?		
When did exports increase?	Two years ago.	
How was the meeting?	It was good.	
Were the customers busy?	Yes, they were.	No, they weren't.
Was she angry?	Yes, she was.	No, she wasn't.

Practice: past simple

1 Rewrite the sentences using the past simple.

1 I usually arrive at the office before 9 o'clock.
Yesterday *I arrived at the office before 9 o'clock.*

2 Exports are increasing sharply.
In 2011 ______________________.

3 I go to the gym every day.
Last week ______________________.

4 I am happy to see you again.
______________________ last night.

5 I study engineering at university.
From 2008 to 2012 ______________________.

2 What did you do yesterday? Write some sentences describing what you did.

____

____

____

____

____

3 Look at these answers to some questions. Write the questions.

Q. ______________________?
A. Yes, they were.

Q. ______________________?
A. Exports increased in 2010.

Q. ______________________?
A. No, they didn't.

Q. ______________________?
A. 10 years ago.

Q. ______________________?
A. Yes, I did.

Q. ______________________?
A. I gave a presentation, then I talked to some customers.

Q. ______________________?
A. I worked in Paris for 10 years.

UNIT 11 Grammar reference

will / be going to

Use *will / won't* for offers and promises.

*I'll send you my application. / I **won't** be late.*

Use *will / won't* for quick decisions about the future.

A: It's raining!

*B: Oh, then I'**ll** take a taxi.*

Use *be going to* for future plans.

*We'**re going to** go to New Zealand this summer.*

Practice: *will / be going to*

1 Complete the sentences with the correct form of the verbs in brackets.

1 He ______________ finish the reports. (not / going to)

2 There's too much traffic. I ______________ be able to get there in time. (not / will)

3 ______________ you ______________ pack your suitcase tonight? (going to)

4 Promise me you ______________ call me when you get there. (will)

5 They said they ______________ lower the price. (will / not)

6 They ______________ attend the seminar. (not / be going to)

2 Circle the correct answer.

1 A: What are you doing this weekend?

B: *I'll have / I'm going to have* a tennis lesson.

2 A: Can you get me the sales report?

B: *I'll get it right away. / I'm going to get it right away.*

3 A: Remember the time difference between here and Sydney.

B: Oh, that's right. OK, *I won't / I'm not going to* call before 9:00am their time.

4 A: I hear you're transferring to Beijing next year.

B: Yes, so *I'll take / I'm going to take* a Chinese Mandarin class.

5 A: I can't get this document to print correctly.

B: Don't worry, *I'll help you / I'm going to help you.*

UNIT 12

Grammar reference

Making and responding to offers

Making offers is a common part of conversation in English. To make an offer, use *Would you like* with a noun or *Would you like / Would you like me* with the infinitive (*to …*).

Would you like	a sandwich? some (more) coffee? to play golf this weekend? to see our new catalogue?
Would you like me to	help you? show you where the room is? carry your bag?

Respond to offers with *Yes, please* or *No, thank you* (we often add a positive comment when accepting an offer, or a reason when refusing).

Yes, please.	I'd love one / some. I'd love to. That would be great.
No, thank you.	I'm fine. I'm sorry, but I can't. I need to work this weekend.

Practice: making and responding to offers

1 Match the offers 1–6 to the responses a–f.

Would you like …

1	some cake?	a	No, thank you. I'm sorry but I can't tomorrow.
2	me to carry that?	b	No, thank you. It's not heavy.
3	to have lunch tomorrow?	c	Yes, please. Which floor is it on?
4	me to send you the report?	d	No, thank you. I'm fine.
5	another cup of coffee?	e	Yes, please. It looks delicious.
6	to see my office?	f	Yes, please. Can you email it to me?

2 Write offers and responses for these situations.

1 Your friend visits your house. It is a hot day and she looks thirsty.

You: Would you like ________________?

Friend: ________________

2 You are sitting on a bus with no empty seats. A young woman gets on the bus carrying a baby.

You: Would you like ________________?

Woman: ________________

3 A foreign businessman is visiting your company. After the meeting he has no plans in the evening.

You: Would you like ________________?

Visitor: ________________

4 You see some tourists looking at a map in front of the train station.

You: Would you like ________________?

Tourist: ________________

Macmillan Education
Between Towns Road, Oxford OX4 3PP
A division of Macmillan Publishers Limited
Companies and representatives throughout the world

ISBN: 978-0-230-43325-0 (TOEIC edition)
ISBN: 978-0-230-44786-8 (BEC edition)

BEC practice material written by Michael Black

First edition published 2008
This edition published 2013

Designed by Carolyn Gibson

Page make-up by Carolyn Gibson

Illustrated by Nigel Dobbyn, Peter Harper, Gregory Roberts and Paul Williams

Cover design by Carolyn Gibson

Cover photographs: Getty

Extracts from the *Macmillan English Dictionary* second edition published 2007 © Macmillan Publishers Limited 2007.

The authors wish to extend their thanks to all those who contributed to this book with their generous advice and assistance. We would especially like to thank our colleagues, management, and students (past and present) at Sumitomo Electric Industries, Sumitomo Metal Industries, Sumikin-Intercom, and other companies, for giving us the experience we needed and for trying out many of the ideas in this book.

Printed and bound in Thailand

2017 2016 2015 2014 2013

10 9 8 7 6 5 4 3 2 1

For assistance with information about international business customs, cross-cultural communication, and the TOEIC: Brett Berquist, Tammy Gilbert, Peiya Gu, Alan Headbloom, Lewis Lansford, Shinji Okumura, Bruce Rogers, Jaimie Scanlon, Tadao Seo, Lynn Stafford-Yilmaz, Kelly Tavares, Gregg Stevens, Kay Westerfield, Tatyana Yahkontova

Thanks to everyone at Macmillan for their support and guidance in the development of this book.

Finally – thanks to our families for their patience and support: Hiroko, Sarah, and Thomas Vaughan; and Will and Sebastian Mitchell.

The authors and publishers would like to thank the following for permission to reproduce their photographs: **Alamy Images** p62tl; Alamy/ PanaromaMedia p.47(r); **Art Directors and Trip** p10(tm); **Bananastock** pp16(tl), 16(r), P22(tm), 25(r), 25(l), 27(tm),28(m), 36(tr), 40, 42(tr), 46(l), 62(tm), 68(tm), 80(tr), 112(l), 34(r), 46(r), 80(breakfast), 80(watching TV), 80(party); **Corbis** p114(r); **Digital Vision** pp28(r), 62(tr), 62(r); **Getty Images/Stone/Siri Stafford** p80tl; **Image Source** pp10(tl), 10(tr), P22(tr), 16(tm), 36(tm), 42(tl), 42(tm), 47(l), 54(tm), 54(tr), 68(tl), 68(tr), 108(l), 110(l), 110(r), 112(r), 114(l); 116(r) 118(r), 22(br), 34(l), 80(sports); **istock/Tatian popova** p8; **Photodisc** p99; **Photolibrary.com** p28(tl); **Photoalto** p87; **Punchstock** pp22(bm), P22(tl), 80(tm); 80(dessert), 80(unhappy), 81; **Stockbyte** pp22(bl), 108(r), 116(l), 118(l); **Thinkstock** pp36(tl), 54(tl).

References to photographs on pages 108-119 refer to the TOEIC edition.